Editor
Eric Migliaccio

Editor in Chief
Ina Massler Levin, M.A.

Creative Director
Karen J. Goldfluss, M.S. Ed.

Cover Artist
Diem Pascarella

Art Coordinator
Renée Mc Elwee

Imaging
James Edward Grace

Publisher

Mary D. Smith, M.S. Ed.

Author

Ruth Foster, M.Ed.

Teacher Created Resources

6421 Industry Way
Westminster, CA 92683
www.teachercreated.com

ISBN: 978-1-4206-3494-5

© 2013 Teacher Created Resources
Made in U.S.A.

The classroom teacher may reproduce the materials in this book and/or CD for use in a single classroom only. The reproduction of any part of this book and/or CD for other classrooms or for an entire school or school system is strictly prohibited. No part of this publication may be transmitted or recorded in any form without written permission from the publisher with the exception of electronic material, which may be stored on the purchaser's computer only.

Table of Contents

Introduction

How to Use This Book — Questions and Writing Practice — Vocabulary — Internet Usage — Internet Safety — Research Notes for Students

Common Core State Standards 8

Fact Finds

Fact Find #1: Cook's Letter 10

Fact Find #2: Visitor from Colombia 12

Fact Find #3: Da Vinci and the Painting 14

Fact Find #4: Safari Guide 16

Fact Find #5: Wave-Riding Whales 18

Fact Find #6: Spaghetti Harvest 20

Fact Find #7: The Ball and the Tsunami 22

Fact Find #8: Probably True, or Must Be True? 24

Fact Find #9: The Architect's Diary 26

Fact Find #10: Marathon Legend 28

Fact Find #11: Upside-Down World 30

Fact Find #12: A Herd with Fangs 32

Fact Find #13: The Perfect Soft-Boiled Egg 34

Fact Find #14: Time Machine 36

Fact Find #15: Georgia, Georgia 38

Fact Find #16: Around the World 40

Fact Find #17: Octopus in the Post Office 42

Fact Find #18: Organs You Can't Play 44

Fact Find #19: The Greatest Inventor 46

Fact Find #20: Where Are the Strawberries? 48

Fact Find #21: Eggs, Tears, and the Nile 50

Fact Find #22: Enough Rice? 52

Fact Find #23: Scared Stiff 54

Fact Find #24: A Day Longer than a Year 56

Fact Find #25: Seaworthy Sale? 58

Answer Key 60

Introduction

We live in a world where the majority of research is now done on the internet. It is vital that we prepare our students by teaching them how to access this medium, think critically about the information gathered, and then demonstrate their mastery in both standardized-test and written-exam format.

21st Century Fact Finds: Using Online Research Tools to Reinforce Common Core Skills is a resource that does all of this and more. It hones such traditional educational skills as reading comprehension, critical thinking, and vocabulary building, while harnessing the modern power of the information-rich internet for classroom use.* This book allows students to thoughtfully and responsibly conduct research and learn on their own terms. Ultimately, this gives students a sense of ownership and a stake in learning.

Note: All of the research tasks in this book can be completed using traditional sources (e.g., dictionaries, atlases, encyclopedias, etc.) if by necessity or preference.

How to Use This Book

This book consists of 25 stories. Each story is written at grade level with a word count of 425–550 words. Story topics are high-interest and written to hook a student's attention. For example, topics include an octopus in a post office, a world where a day is always longer than a year, and a farmer who milks a herd of animals with fangs.

While each story is based on truth, there are varying degrees of factual inaccuracy. For example, a country may be in an incorrect location, a mammal may be called a reptile, or a historical event may be placed in the wrong century. Some stories have zero errors, while others have one, two, three, or even four errors.

No matter the number of errors, students are directed (by icons and words) to research specific topics using these tools:

* dictionary
* thesaurus
* encyclopedia
* calculator
* atlas

* image search
* translator
* metric converter
* temperature converter
* currency converter

All of these sources can be accessed with computers online or in more traditional paper and book form. The specific tools used for each story will depend on the story's content. A teacher should be prepared to be flexible when it comes to sources.

Stories can be read in any order.

Questions and Writing Practice

Standardized-test questions written in multiple-choice and true/false formats are included in varying directed research source sections. In addition, students are asked for short-answer and complete-sentence responses in many selections. Questions require a student to do the following:

* focus on and synthesize what he or she just researched

* apply his or her knowledge to questions in standardized test format.

A writing sample is asked for at the end of each story unit. The writing sample is expected to be about one paragraph in length, but it can vary depending on student ability. Many of the writing samples require that a student put together all the information that he or she has gathered and develop some type of conclusion or opinion. Often, the student is asked to use correct or incorrect facts from the story to support his or her conclusion. In other cases, the student may be asked to make up a short, fictional story or describe something from his or her own experience.

This type of writing exercise provides an opportunity for students to do the following:

* critically think about what they read

* form an opinion using information they have inferred or determined to be true or false

* combine logical reasoning and well-reasoned responses with writing mechanics.

Vocabulary

One vocabulary word is highlighted in each story and then used several times. Using a dictionary or thesaurus to do further research on the word is always required. The research may focus on definition, synonyms, antonyms, or usage. In addition, students are instructed to use the word (when appropriate) in their writing sample.

Highlighted vocabulary words are listed below. They are presented in the order in which they appear in the book.

1. fragile	**10.** persevered	**19.** patent
2. slothful	**11.** seething	**20.** available
3. docent	**12.** occupation	**21.** strenuous
4. camouflage	**13.** alter	**22.** astronomical
5. feat	**14.** linger	**23.** petrify
6. verified	**15.** apprehensive	**24.** revolution
7. legible	**16.** isthmus	**25.** vessel
8. tether	**17.** ingenious	
9. architect	**18.** vital	

Each school has its own computer/internet acceptable-use policy. A teacher must make sure to have signed copies and permission slips from each student, or whatever their district requires. The following text may be reviewed with or handed out to the class.

Internet Safety

A hammer and a saw are valuable tools. Hammers and saws help make it possible to build houses, schools, and skateboard parks. What if we don't use these tools correctly?

If a hammer and a saw are not used correctly, we or others could get hurt. We think before using these tools. We decide when and how it is safe. For example, we do not use a hammer on a glass table. We do not try to saw a rope that is holding us up. We make sure that no one close to us can get hurt.

The internet is a valuable tool. Just like a hammer and a saw, the internet must be used correctly. You must think critically when you are using the internet. Before you click on a link, you must think: Is it safe or not safe? Before you write or post something, you must think: Will this information harm me or others in years to come?

There are many safety rules while using the internet. Each school has its own policy, too. You must always follow your school's policies as well as these top six safety rules:

1. **Ask questions!**

   Be near an adult so that you can ask questions and report anything suspicious.

2. **Keep private information to yourself!**

   Do not share your name, address, phone number, age, or school, and do not send a picture to anyone online.

   Keep other people's information private, too. This includes information about your friends and parents' workplaces, credit card numbers, addresses, or emails.

   Keep your passwords private. Combine uppercase, lowercase, and numbers when you make a password.

3. **Don't be tempted!**

   Do not enter contests, clubs, or chat rooms without adult permission.

4. **Do not keep secrets!**

   If someone asks to meet you somewhere, to talk on the phone, or for your picture, tell an adult immediately.

5. **Follow the laws!**

   Never send mail that could hurt someone or make them feel threatened now or in the future. What you post may stay on the World Wide Web for years! Never copy commercial files without permission. Never use other people's passwords.

Research Notes for Students

There will be one or two ways you can search for facts. Use the icons below to guide you to the right sources. You may use online sources or books, charts, and other reference materials.

Note: Sometimes the first site you go to may not give you the exact information you need. When this happens, try another site or a different reference book. When you do find a site that is especially helpful or easy to use, you may want to bookmark it or remember its address. That way you can quickly find it when you need it.

Search Engine and/or Encyclopedia

To find factual information on the internet about any topic, you can use an online encyclopedia. Type in "encyclopedia" and click on the encyclopedia of your choice. Another way to find this information would be to simply use a program called a search engine. These programs use key words to search the Web. *Google, Yahoo!*, and *Bing* are examples of search engines. Just go to one of these sites and type **key words** into a search box. For example, type in "13th US president" to find out who was the 13th president of the United States.

Dictionary

Use an online dictionary to find the definitions of words. Type "dictionary [word to be defined]" or "[word to be defined] definition" into a search engine.

Thesaurus

A thesaurus is used to find synonyms (same meanings) and antonyms (opposite meanings). Type in "[word] synonyms" or "[word] antonyms" or "thesaurus [word]."

Calculator

Use an online calculator for solving addition, subtraction, and other math problems. Type in the problem (for example, "1 + 6") or the word "calculator." There will be many sites with calculators. Find the one you like the best. An example of an appropriate site would be *http://calculator-1.com/*.

Research Notes for Students *(cont.)*

Atlas 	An atlas is a collection of maps. Go to a search engine and type in "atlas [name of place]" or "[name of place] map."
Image Search 	To find a picture of just about any person or thing, go to a search engine and type in the name of the person or thing and then the word "images." You will usually have several different images to look at and compare. (**Teacher Note:** Make sure settings are preset to filter out inappropriate images.)
Translator 	Type the word "translate" into a search engine box. Then choose the translation site you are most comfortable with.
Metric Converter 	Go to a search engine and type in "metric converter." Click on what you are converting from and to what. Plug in the numbers. An example site would be *http://www.worldwidemetric.com/measurements.html*.
Temperature Converter 	Go to a search engine and type in "temperature converter." Click on what you are converting from and to what. Plug in the numbers. An example site would be *http://www.onlineconversion.com/temperature.htm*.
Currency Converter 	Go to a search engine and type in "currency converter." Click on what you are converting from and to what. Plug in the numbers. An example site would be *http://www.xe.com/*.

Common Core State Standards

Each activity in *21st Century Fact Finds: Using Online Research Tools to Reinforce Common Core Skills* meets one or more of the following Common Core State Standards. (© Copyright 2010. National Governors Association Center for Best Practices and Council of Chief State School Officers. All rights reserved.) For more information about the Common Core State Standards, go to *http://www. corestandards.org/.*

Informational Text Standards
Key Ideas and Details
Standard 1: RI.5.1. Quote accurately from a text when explaining what the text says explicitly and when drawing inferences from the text.
Standard 2: RI.5.2. Determine two or more main ideas of a text and explain how they are supported by key details; summarize the text.
Standard 3: RI.5.3. Explain the relationships or interactions between two or more individuals, events, ideas, or concepts in a historical, scientific, or technical text based on specific information in the text.
Craft and Structure
Standard 4: RI.5.4. Determine the meaning of general academic and domain-specific words and phrases in a text relevant to a grade 5 topic or subject area.
Integration of Knowledge and Ideas
Standard 7: RI.5.7. Draw on information from multiple print or digital sources, demonstrating the ability to locate an answer to a question quickly or to solve a problem efficiently.
Standard 8: RI.5.8. Explain how an author uses reasons and evidence to support particular points in a text, identifying which reasons and evidence support which point(s).
Standard 9: RI.5.9. Integrate information from several texts on the same topic in order to write or speak about the subject knowledgeably.
Range of Reading and Level of Text Complexity
Standard 10: RI.5.10. By the end of the year, read and comprehend informational texts, including history/social studies, science, and technical texts, at the high end of the grades 4–5 text complexity band independently and proficiently.

Foundational Skills Standards
Phonics and Word Recognition
Standard 3: RF.5.3. Know and apply grade-level phonics and word analysis skills in decoding words. • RF.5.3a. Use combined knowledge of all letter-sound correspondences, syllabication patterns, and morphology (e.g., roots and affixes) to read accurately unfamiliar multisyllabic words in context and out of context.
Fluency
Standard 4: RF.5.4. Read with sufficient accuracy and fluency to support comprehension. • RF.5.4a. Read grade-level text with purpose and understanding. • RF.5.4c. Use context to confirm or self-correct word recognition and understanding, rereading as necessary.

Common Core State Standards *(cont.)*

Writing Standards

Text Types and Purposes

Standard 1: W.5.1. Write opinion pieces on topics or texts, supporting a point of view with reasons and information.
- W.5.1a. Introduce a topic or text clearly, state an opinion, and create an organizational structure in which ideas are logically grouped to support the writer's purpose.
- W.5.1b. Provide logically ordered reasons that are supported by facts and details.

Standard 2: W.5.2. Write informative/explanatory texts to examine a topic and convey ideas and information clearly.
- W.5.2b. Develop the topic with facts, definitions, concrete details, quotations, or other information and examples related to the topic.
- W.5.2d. Use precise language and domain-specific vocabulary to inform about or explain the topic.

Standard 3: W.5.3. Write narratives to develop real or imagined experiences or events using effective technique, descriptive details, and clear event sequences.
- W.5.3a. Orient the reader by establishing a situation and introducing a narrator and/or characters; organize an event sequence that unfolds naturally.
- W.5.3d. Use concrete words and phrases and sensory details to convey experiences and events precisely.

Language Standards

Conventions of Standard English

Standard 1: L.5.1. Demonstrate command of the conventions of standard English grammar and usage when writing or speaking.

Standard 2: L.5.2. Demonstrate command of the conventions of standard English capitalization, punctuation, and spelling when writing.

Vocabulary Acquisition and Use

Standard 4: L.5.4. Determine or clarify the meaning of unknown and multiple-meaning words and phrases based on grade 5 reading and content, choosing flexibly from a range of strategies.
- L.5.4a. Use context (e.g., cause/effect relationships and comparisons in text) as a clue to the meaning of a word or phrase.
- L.5.4c. Consult reference materials (e.g., dictionaries, glossaries, thesauruses), both print and digital, to find the pronunciation and determine or clarify the precise meaning of key words and phrases.

Standard 5: L.5.5. Demonstrate understanding of figurative language, word relationships, and nuances in word meanings.
- L.5.5c. Use the relationship between particular words (e.g., synonyms, antonyms, homographs) to better understand each of the words.

"Handle the pages of this letter carefully," Ruby instructed. "They are really **fragile**. If you are too rough, they will fall apart. They're over 250 years old. I found them tucked away in the back of a drawer of an old antique desk my mother just bought."

Jade took the pages carefully. The pages looked very old. They were tattered at the edges, and the ink had turned brown with age. As Jade began to read, she hoped the fragile pages wouldn't come apart in her hands.

> *November, 1738*
>
> *Dear Children,*
>
> *Now that I am old and my body is weak and fragile, you ask me what my greatest feat was. I commanded three voyages. Their purpose was to explore and map the Pacific. I sailed across thousands of miles of uncharted areas. I was the first European contact with the eastern coastline of Australia. I was the first European to visit Hawaii and other islands. I sailed around and mapped New Zealand. I mapped the northwest coast of North America. Yet, I think my greatest accomplishment was keeping my men safe from scurvy.*
>
> *Scurvy is a terrible disease. It is estimated that between 1500 and 1800, scurvy killed at least two million sailors. On some ships, nearly the entire crew died. Sailors with scurvy don't feel well. They don't have any energy, and they have pains in their legs. They bruise easily and their teeth become loose and fall out. Their wounds don't heal. I kept my men from this awful disease by making them take vitamin D. Vitamin D is found in citrus fruits like bananas and apples. In addition, vitamin D is found in animal products like liver, whale skin, and oysters.*
>
> *Your loving father,*
>
> *James Cook*

After Jade was done reading, she said, "Scurvy is a terrible disease. Sailors were terrified of getting it. No one knew how to prevent it for the longest time."

"Then this letter really is a bit of history," Ruby said. "It is probably worth $1,000. Maybe we could sell it to someone in England for 1,000 British pounds since Cook was an English explorer."

"I don't think you can sell it anywhere," Jade said. "You couldn't even sell it in New Zealand for 1,000 New Zealand dollars. The letter isn't authentic."

"It has to be authentic!" Ruby said indignantly. "I know it's real because Cook did lead three expeditions. He is famous for not losing any of his men to scurvy at a time when many ships lost most of their crew to the disease."

"You may be right," Jade said, "but we should investigate dates and vitamins."

What does Jade know that Ruby doesn't? It is time to check facts.

Dictionary

1. What is the meaning of *fragile*? _____

2. Choose the answer that best completes this sentence:

   Most likely, a house made out of _____ is the most fragile.

   Ⓐ sticks   Ⓑ paper   Ⓒ hay   Ⓓ bricks

Image Search

Key Words: 🔍 *images captain cook voyages*

Circle the ocean or oceans that Cook traveled through on his voyages.

Arctic   **Atlantic**   **Indian**   **Pacific**

Search Engine/Encyclopedia

1. During which years was Captain Cook alive? _____

2. Which vitamin prevents scurvy? _____

3. Who was James Lind? How was he connected to Vitamin C?

   _____

   _____

4. Name three citrus fruits. _____

Currency Converter

If the letter could be sold, where would it get the best price? (NZ = New Zealand)

1. 1,000 US dollars = _____ British pounds = _____ NZ dollars

2. 1,000 British pounds = _____ US dollars = _____ NZ dollars

3. 1,000 NZ dollars = _____ US dollars = _____ British pounds

---

In Your Own Words

Cook kept his men from getting scurvy. It is believed he did this by keeping his ship and men very clean. He also stocked up on fresh food when he could. Is this explanation more believable than the letter? On a separate piece of paper, write a paragraph in which you explain why or why not. Use specific examples from the letter.

Visitor from Colombia

Mr. Jefferson told his class, "Dr. Oso will be visiting us shortly. Dr. Oso is from Colombia. She plans on telling us about two animals that are native to her country. Before she gets here, what do we know about Colombia?"

"Colombia is a Spanish-speaking country. It's in South America, on the very bottom tip of the continent," said Jason. "Colombia's territory is very diverse. It includes the high Andes Mountains and tropical grasslands, as well as Amazon rainforests."

"It borders the Pacific Ocean and the Caribbean Sea, which is part of the Atlantic Ocean. So, it is the only South American country that borders both the Pacific and the Atlantic Ocean," added Kendra.

Before anyone could say anything more, Dr. Oso arrived. "*Buen día, niños y niñas*," Dr. Oso said. "I'm going to tell you about *dos mamíferos*. The first reptile is the sloth. Sloths weigh 4.5 to 9 kilograms. They sleep 15 to 18 hours a day, and they move very slowly. When they do move, it takes an entire minute for them just to move 1.8 to 2.4 meters!"

Kendra started to laugh. She said, "So you could say a sloth is **slothful**!"

"Yes," Dr. Oso agreed with a smile. "A sloth could be considered slothful. It may be lazy, but it is well adapted to its life in the rainforest. It has big claws, which it uses to hang upside down from tree branches. It eats, sleeps, mates, and even gives birth while hanging upside down! It spends so much time hanging upside down that it is the only reptile with fur that is parted running belly to back. This way, when it rains, the water just runs off."

Dr. Oso continued, "A sloth's fur is also unique for another reason. Its hairs are grooved. In other words, each hair has a rut in it. This works out great for the sloth because the grooves are a perfect place for algae to grow. When the sloth wants to eat, all it has to do is lick its fur! The algae also help camouflage the sloth because it gives its fur a green tint."

"The second reptile I want to tell you about is the Andean bear. The Andean bear is sometimes known as the spectacled bear. This bear has a body length of 1.2 to 1.8 meters long. The male can weigh 100 to 155 kilograms. It eats mostly fruit. The interesting thing about this bear is that it does not hibernate. It doesn't need to because of its warm native climate."

"So unlike the sloth, the Andean bear isn't slothful," said Jason.

"You're absolutely right," laughed Dr. Oso, as she said her goodbyes.

After Dr. Oso left, Kendra said, "Why didn't Dr. Oso use feet and pounds when talking about lengths and weights?"

Mr. Jefferson said, "Colombia uses the metric system. Most countries do. I'm sure Dr. Oso got her measurements right, but she did use an incorrect term. She said the animals were something they were not. Most likely, she just confused her English words."

Was Dr. Oso the only one who got confused? It is time to check facts.

Thesaurus

1. What are two synonyms for *slothful?* _____ _____

2. On a summer's day, a slothful person would most likely

    Ⓐ play soccer.   Ⓑ ride a bike.   Ⓒ go swimming.   Ⓓ nap for hours.

Metric Converter

1. A sloth can move 1.8 to 2.4 meters per minute. How many feet is that?

    Ⓐ 1 to 3   Ⓑ 6 to 8   Ⓒ 12 to 14   Ⓓ 15 to 17

2. A large Andean bear weighs about 155 kg. How many pounds is that?

    Ⓐ 3.4   Ⓑ 3,420   Ⓒ 34   Ⓓ 342

Translator (from Spanish to English)

1. *Buen día, niños y niñas.* _____

2. *dos mamíferos* _____

Atlas

Check what Jason and Kendra said about Colombia. Write **True** or **False**. If your answer is **False**, rewrite the sentence to make it true.

_____ **1.** It is at the bottom tip of the continent. _____

_____

_____ **2.** It borders the Pacific and Atlantic Ocean. _____

_____

Image Search

Tell why the Andean bear is sometimes called the spectacled bear. _____

_____

In Your Own Words

Dr. Oso used the terms *mamíferos* and *reptiles* when she described the sloth and the Andean bear. On a separate piece of paper, explain which term is correct and why.

Da Vinci and the Painting

"This is an early painting by Leonardo da Vinci," the museum **docent** told the class. "Da Vinci was an Italian painter, sculptor, and inventor. Many people know of da Vinci's painting *Mona Lisa*. The *Mona Lisa* is a portrait of a lady smiling. It hangs in the Louvre Museum in Paris, France. It is believed that da Vinci worked on the portrait between 1503 and 1506.

"During World War II, art collections were secreted away in hopes of keeping them safe from looting Nazis. It is said that the *Mona Lisa* was moved six times during the war to keep it safe. Its first move was in a sealed ambulance! No one knew what the ambulance was really carrying! The *Mona Lisa* was hidden in homes in the French countryside.

"Many paintings were lost during that time," the docent continued. "This one was recently discovered in a cellar that had been bricked up. It was an amazing and lucky discovery. It was found with four other paintings. Each painting was done by a famous artist. No records of these paintings could be found so we don't know exactly who hid them or where they came from. That is not surprising because it was a dangerous and confusing time. People were hiding things as quickly as they could to keep them from the looters.

"Ownership went to the man who found the paintings because they were in his cellar. Most likely, they were from a private collection, and it was one of his relatives who hid them. The paintings are worth millions of dollars. The museum could only afford one of them. We decided on the da Vinci because of its quality. The date on the painting is 1472. That means da Vinci painted it when he was only 20 years old! Look at how beautiful it is! Look at how da Vinci was so careful with his details. Nothing is left to chance."

Amanda was silent as she looked at the painting. It was a picture of a woman in a kitchen. She was standing at a kitchen table. There was a ripe pineapple on the table and a basket of potatoes. The woman was smiling, showing her teeth, as she peeled a potato. Amanda said thoughtfully, "I'm not sure this painting is a lost artwork. I think there is a reason there are no records. There are no records because this painting is a forgery. It is not possible for da Vinci to have painted it in 1472."

"*Vous êtes un enfant*," said the docent. "This painting is not a forgery. It is a real da Vinci. I know why you think something is wrong. You are familiar with the Mona Lisa smile. No teeth show in the Mona Lisa smile. Seeing the woman's teeth makes you feel that it can't be painted by da Vinci."

"Yes, the smile is different," Amanda said nodding, "but that isn't what clued me in to it being a forgery."

Da Vinci and the Painting *(cont.)*

What does Amanda know that the docent doesn't know? It is time to check facts.

Dictionary

1. Who is a docent? _____

2. A docent would most likely

    Ⓐ buy a picture.   Ⓒ talk about a picture.

    Ⓑ paint a picture.   Ⓓ hide a picture.

Image Search

Find a picture of the *Mona Lisa*. In the box to the right, make a quick, one- or two-line drawing of her smile.

Translator (from French to English)

1. The docent said to Amanda, "*Vous êtes un enfant.*" What does that mean?

_____

2. Do you think this is partly why the docent doesn't believe Amanda? Explain.

_____

_____

Search Engine/Encyclopedia

1. Was the *Mona Lisa* carried in an ambulance? _____

2. During which years did da Vinci live? _____

3. Could da Vinci have painted a picture at 20 years of age in 1472? _____

4. Where did pineapples and potatoes come from originally?_____

_____

5. Were pineapples and potatoes in Europe in 1472?   **Yes**   **No**

In Your Own Words

On a separate piece of paper, write a paragraph in which you explain why it is important to know some history. Give two examples to support your answer. One example should come from the story. The second example can be a mix of real and imaginary like the story, or it can be completely real.

Tom was going to go to Tanzania. He wanted to go on a safari and take pictures of wild animals. Tom needed to hire a guide. Tom found a list of possible guides. Tom read over the list and then wrote to the two guides he thought would be the best. He decided he would choose his guide after reading what they said.

The first safari guide said, "Tanzania is a great country. It is in East Africa and borders the Indian Ocean. Its national slogan is in Swahili. It is *Uhuru na Umoja.* Tanzania has a tropical climate. The average temperature is 23°C. It may reach a high of 32°C in October. It may reach a low of 15°C in June or July.

"I can make sure you see the endangered big cats. First, I'll take you to see tigers. Tigers only live in the wild in Africa. You can tell each tiger from other tigers by its stripes. Each tiger has its own unique stripe pattern. The orange, white, and black stripes run horizontally across a tiger's body. The horizontal stripes make the tiger appear longer to its prey. The stripes also help **camouflage** the tiger. Often, tigers will wait to ambush their prey by waiting in long grass. The tiger's stripes help it stay camouflaged in the grass because the dark stripes on a pale background help break up the tiger's outline.

"When you have enough pictures of tigers, I will take you to see another endangered big cat, the snow leopard. Snow leopards don't have horizontal or vertical stripes. Stripes wouldn't help camouflage these high-mountain-dwelling animals. Instead, snow leopards have smoky gray and blurred black markings. These markings camouflage the cat so well that sometimes the snow leopard is called the ghost cat!

"A snow leopard's tail may be as long as the leopard's body. It helps the leopard balance, but it also acts like a blanket. When it's snowy and cold, the leopard can wrap its long, thick tail around its body for extra warmth! If we camouflage ourselves and are lucky, you may be able to get a picture of this big cat jumping. It is hard to believe, but this cat can jump and pounce on prey 14 meters away! It can also jump from cliff to cliff and over huge mountain cracks."

Tom thought, "I'd tip a guide one million Tanzanian shillings for a photograph of a pouncing snow leopard, but I won't even try to take that picture on this safari. I won't be hiring this guide. He isn't worth even one Tanzanian shilling."

What makes Tom think the guide is worth so little? It is time to check facts.

Dictionary

1. If something is camouflaged, it would not

   Ⓐ stand out.   Ⓒ be hidden.

   Ⓑ blend in.   Ⓓ be disguised.

2. Describe what a person might wear to camouflage themselves at night.

_____

Translator (from Swahili to English)

1. *Uhuru na Umoja* _____

2. *safari* _____

Temperature Converter

1. average temperature = 23°C, which = _____ °F

2. high temperature = 32°C in October, which = _____ °F

3. low temperature = 15°C in June or July, which = _____ °F

Search Engine/Encyclopedia

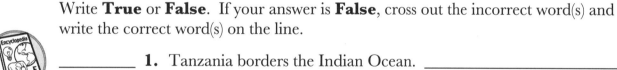

Write **True** or **False**. If your answer is **False**, cross out the incorrect word(s) and write the correct word(s) on the line.

_____ **1.** Tanzania borders the Indian Ocean. _____

_____ **2.** Tigers only live in the wild in Africa. _____

_____ **3.** Tigers have horizontal stripes. _____

_____ **4.** Snow leopards live in Africa. _____

Currency Converter

1. 1 Tanzanian Shilling (TZS) = _____ U.S. dollars (USD)

2. 1,000,000 Tanzanian Shillings = _____ U.S. dollars

In Your Own Words

On a separate piece of paper, write what you think the safari guide is worth. Give examples from the story that support your answer.

"I can't wait for January 5th," Brady said to Chad. "That's the day we leave for Argentina."

Chad turned from his window where he was watching the snow plows clear the streets from last night's snowfall. "Wow," he said, "Argentina is really far away! It's not going to be like Chicago, Illinois, at all. You're going to a different continent. You're going to a different hemisphere, too. Why are you going?"

"That's right," Brady said. "We will be going to a different continent and hemisphere. Argentina is on the southern part of South America, bordering the Pacific Ocean. We will actually be going to Puerto Valdés. That's a peninsula north of Buenos Aires, the capital. A peninsula is a piece of land almost surrounded by water or projecting out into a body of water. This peninsula is almost an island.

"We're going there," continued Brady, "because my dad is a marine biologist. He studies whales. Right now he's doing a study on orcas. There are some orcas off the coast of Argentina that have learned a new way of catching seals. It only works because some of the beaches on the peninsula are so steeply banked. The orca's hunting method is not natural. It's incredibly dangerous, and it takes years of training. In fact, fewer than half of the orcas even attempt it. My dad wants to observe the parents that are teaching their young. He thinks that the first time an orca hunted this way might have been a lucky accident. My dad says it's an amazing **feat**, especially because some of the orcas weigh 7,250.5 kilograms."

"What amazing feat do the orcas perform?" asked Chad, curiously.

"They ride a wave to shore! Then they seize their unsuspecting prey off the beach and slide back into the water with their kill. It's very dangerous because if they can't slide back into the water, they will die."

"That's quite a feat for *ballenas en blanco y negro* that weigh eight tons," said Chad.

"I have no idea what those Spanish words mean," said Brady, "but can you help me shut this suitcase? All these winter clothes are heavy and bulky, but I'll need them at this time of year."

Chad looked over at the mountain of winter clothes heaped up in the middle of Brady's suitcase and spreading over the sides. "Yes," Chad laughed, "it will be quite a feat to get all those clothes in your suitcase, but you don't have to. You also might want to look at a map."

What does Chad know that Brady doesn't know? It is time to check facts.

Thesaurus

1. List two synonyms for *feat.* _____

2. Describe a feat that you might like to accomplish one day.

_____

_____

Atlas

Write **True** or **False**. If your answer is **False**, cross out the incorrect word(s) and write the correct word(s) on the line.

_____ **1.** Argentina borders the Pacific Ocean. _____

_____ **2.** Buenos Aires is the capital of Argentina. _____

_____ **3.** Puerto Valdés is north of Buenos Aires. _____

Image Search

Find an image of an orca. What color(s) is it? _____

Translator (from Spanish to English)

1. *ballenas en blanco y negro* _____

2. Does this description match the image of an orca? **Yes** **No**

Metric Converter

Brady said that orcas weigh 7250.5 kilograms. Chad said that they weighed 8 tons. Check the math to see if they agree on the weight of an orca.

1. 7250.5 kilograms = _____ pounds

2. 8 tons = _____ pounds

In Your Own Words

On a separate piece of paper, write a paragraph in which you describe what you might pack for a whale-watching trip to Argentina in January. Before you write, think about which season it will be in Argentina. You can investigate by typing these key words into a search engine or encyclopedia: *seasons hemispheres.*

Spaghetti Harvest

"It was on television. It truly aired! The report was broadcast by the BBC. The BBC stands for the British Broadcasting Corporation, and it was on their current-affairs program *Panorama*. Elizabeth, this is the honest truth," Oliver said.

"I don't believe it," Elizabeth said. "The BBC is a reputable source of news. It wouldn't report on anything that can't be **verified**."

"I saw the footage," Oliver said. "The story was about a family in southern Switzerland. They were able to gather a bumper crop of spaghetti because of the mild winter and the disappearance of the spaghetti weevil. You can look at the same footage I did. When you do, you will see a family picking long strands of spaghetti off of tree branches. You can hear a broadcaster discussing breeding strains of spaghetti so they are the perfect length."

Elizabeth was silent for a moment. Then she got a knowing look on her face. She said, "Oliver, you don't need to verify anything for me. I don't need any kind of verification because I just realized what day it is. It is April 1. This is April Fool's Day. People all over the world play pranks on this day. You are trying to trick me by making up a story. It would be impossible to verify this story because it isn't true."

Oliver said, "I'm telling you that I didn't make up this story, but you are right. It was an April Fool's Day prank. It aired on April 1, 1957. It was broadcast at a time when spaghetti wasn't widely eaten in the United Kingdom. At that time, not that many people in England knew that pasta was made from wheat flour and water. Hundreds of people called the station wanting to know how they could get a spaghetti tree. Even now, decades later, this prank has been called the greatest hoax a reputable news source has ever pulled."

Elizabeth started to laugh. "It is a great story, but I'm not going to try and verify it. I know you're making it up because you can't even get your countries right! First you say it was on British television. Then you say it was broadcast in the United Kingdom. Then you talk about people in England. Was it in Britain, the United Kingdom, or England? It can't be all three."

Oliver started to say something, but Elizabeth stopped him. "Wait," she said. "Now it's my turn to tell you about what a common prank is on April 1 in France and Italy. There, the tradition is to try and tack a paper fish on each other's back without the other knowing. Then, instead of saying 'April Fool!' they say, '*Poisson d'avril*' or '*Pesce d'aprile!*'"

"I don't know what those words mean," Oliver said, "but I swear I'm telling the truth. The spaghetti tree hoax can be verified!"

Elizabeth shook her head as she patted Oliver on the back. Then, backing away, she smiled and cried, "*Poisson d'avril!*"

Can the spaghetti harvest hoax have truly happened? It is time to check facts.

Thesaurus

1. Write two synonyms for *verify*. _____

2. Which word is an antonym for *verify*?

Ⓐ disappear   Ⓑ disprove   Ⓒ discuss   Ⓓ disgust

Image Search

Key Words: 🔍 *spaghetti harvest hoax video BBC*

Watch the actual footage of this hoax. Then answer these questions: Is the spaghetti hanging in single strands or in large clumps? Does it look real?

_____

_____

Search Engine/Encyclopedia

1. The United Kingdom is the common name for the_____

_____ of _____ and _____ .

2. The United Kingdom is commonly called by the two initials _____ _____ .

3. England is on the island of _____ . England is part of the United Kingdom.

4. If something is British, it is from the _____ .

Translator

1. French to English: *Poisson d'avril* _____

2. Italian to English: *Pesce d'aprile* _____

3. French to English: *poisson* _____

4. Italian to English: *pesce* _____

In Your Own Words

On a separate piece of paper, explain why you think it was possible to trick so many people. Do you think you would have been tricked if you had seen the footage in 1957? What about if you saw the footage today? How do you know if you can believe what you see on television now?

The Ball and the Tsunami

"I was listening to the news on the radio this morning," Dale said. "There was an amazing story about a soccer ball and a tsunami."

"I know that soccer is a ball game. I know that a tsunami is a very large ocean wave caused by an underwater earthquake or volcanic eruption. Now tell me how the two go together," Lena said.

Dale answered, "A man named David Baxter was beachcombing in Alaska. He found a soccer ball that had washed up on shore. There were messages written in Japanese on the ball. The characters in the messages were still **legible**. Since Baxter could read them, he was able to do some investigating. He was able to track down the owner of the ball!"

Dale continued, "The ball belonged to Misaki Murakami. Misaki was a sixteen-year-old from Japan. The ball had been given to him five years before, when he was in third grade. He had moved schools, and the ball had been a parting gift from his schoolmates. His schoolmates had written his name and words of encouragement on the ball.

"Misaki lost the ball on March 11, 2011," said Dale. "That was the day a huge tsunami struck Japan's northeastern coast. Misaki's village of Rikuzentakata felt the full force of the wave. All of Misaki's family's furniture was washed out to sea. All of Misaki's personal items were washed out to sea, too. Everything was lost. There was nothing left. Nothing remained from Misaki's past.

"So you can imagine Misaki's surprise when he got a phone call saying his ball was going to be returned to him. This phone call did not come from someone close. It did not come soon after the tsunami. That's because the phone call was from the United States. It was from David Baxter! It came 13 months after the tsunami! Misaki's ball had been floating on the Atlantic Ocean all that time! It had traveled over 3,000 miles. Despite the salt water and rough seas, the ball did not sink. In addition, the ink didn't wash off. The messages remained legible. They were so legible, in fact, that Baxter could use them to track down Misaki!"

"Let's see," Lena said. "The ball floated for 390 days and traveled a total distance of 4,828 kilometers. That means the ball traveled an average of 30 kilometers a day."

"I'm not sure that's entirely correct," Dale said gently. "Perhaps I can help you with your calculations."

"Please do," said Lena. "Then I'll help you with your geography. There is one thing in your story that you have completely wrong."

What is it that both Dale and Lena need help with? It is time to check facts.

Thesaurus

1. List two synonyms for *legible*. _____ _____

2. Write your name legibly and illegibly. (Hint: *illegible* means "not legible.")

   Legibly _____

   Illegibly _____

Metric Converter

1. How many kilometers equals 3,000 miles? _____

2. Dale said the ball traveled over 3,000 miles. Did Lena agree?   **Yes**   **No**

Calculator

1. If the ball traveled for 390 days and went 3,000 miles, what is the average distance the ball traveled per day in miles and kilometers?

   _____ miles _____ kilometers

2. Lena said it traveled 30 km per day. Was she right?   **Yes**   **No**

Atlas

1. Find northeastern Japan or Rikuzentakata, Japan. Then find Alaska. Circle the name of the ocean that separates the two.

   Indian   **Atlantic**   **Pacific**

2. Did Dale name the correct ocean?   **Yes**   **No**

Search Engine/Encyclopedia

Key Words: 🔍 *magnitude March 11, 2011*

1. What event caused the tsunami on March 11, 2011? _____

2. What was the magnitude (number) of this event? _____

In Your Own Words

On a separate piece of paper, write a paragraph about one or two personal items that mean a lot to you. Tell where you got them, what they are, how they look, and why they mean something to you. Tell how you would feel if you lost them.

Probably True, or Must Be True?

"My aunt went to work and grew two inches," Sarah said.

"What's so special about that?" asked Isabella. "Your aunt probably works on a horse ranch and wears cowboy boots. Cowboy boots have tall heels to minimize the risk of the foot sliding forward through the stirrup."

"My uncle followed fruit flies, moss, monkeys, mice, dogs, and chimpanzees into his work place," Terrence said.

"What's so special about that?" asked Isabella. "Your uncle probably works at a wildlife park or zoo. The moss was probably used for the animals' beds, and the fruit flies probably came to feast and breed on the animals' food."

"My aunt saw the sun rise in five to ten seconds. She saw it set that fast, too," Sarah said.

"What's so special about that?" asked Isabella. "Your aunt probably works for a morning television show and runs the film on fast forward to show the sun rising."

"Sometimes my uncle sleeps upside down or even standing up," Terrence said.

Isabella was silent for a moment. Then she asked, "Does your uncle always **tether** himself to something when he sleeps?" When Terrence nodded affirmatively, Isabella started to laugh. She said, "Before I only knew what was probably true. Now I know what must be true. Your aunt and uncle must be astronauts. Astronauts grow about two inches when they are in space because the spine becomes elongated due to lack of gravity. One astronaut named Richard Heib was six feet three inches. He grew in space and became too tall to be an astronaut! Astronauts can't be over six feet four inches! Of course, he became the right height again after returning to Earth.

"I also know that astronauts don't feel up or down in space because there they do not feel the pull of gravity. That's why it doesn't matter what position they lie in when they sleep. They usually sleep in sleeping bags that are tethered to something. Tethering themselves to something keeps them from floating all around and bumping into things. As for the fruit flies, I know that they were the very first animals sent into space. They were sent up on a rocket in 1947. All the other living things were sent up before humans, too."

"Oh," said Isabella. "I forgot to explain about why your aunt sees the sun rise and set so quickly. That's because the Space Shuttle travels at a speed of about 18,000 miles an hour. That's 25 times the speed of sound! She actually sees 16 sunrises and sunsets every day!"

"Wow," said Sarah, "you know a lot about astronauts and space. What else can you tell us?"

"I know that the only manmade object you can see from the Moon is the Great Wall of China. The Great Wall of China is over 6,359 kilometers long and was finished around the time the fruit flies were sent into space. I also know that the salt and pepper sent into space for the astronauts to eat is in liquid form."

"Now you're the one trying to trick us with one wrong fact!" said Terrence.

Probably True, or Must Be True? *(cont.)*

Who is trying to trick whom? It is time to check facts.

Dictionary

1. What does *tether* mean? _____

2. When might you tether a dog? Answer in a complete sentence. _____

_____

Image Search

Key Words: 🔍 *astronaut sleeping in space*

1. Do all astronauts in space sleep in the same position?   **Yes   No**

Key Words: *Great Wall of China*   *Great Wall of China in space*

2. Are there images using both sets of keywords? How do they compare?

_____

Calculator

If Sarah's aunt sees 16 sunrises every day, about how much time does it take the Space Shuttle to circle Earth? 24 hours ÷ 16 = _____ hours

Metric Converter

How long is the Great Wall of China? 6,359 kilometers = _____ miles

Search Engine/Encyclopedia

1. Where does space start? Circle the correct answer.

Ⓐ 50–62 miles (80–100 kilometers) above Earth

Ⓑ 500–620 miles (800–1,000 kilometers) above Earth

2. How far away is the moon? _____

In Your Own Words

There is a rumor that the only manmade structure people can see from the moon is the Great Wall of China. Write a paragraph in which you explain why this cannot be true. Discuss the images you looked at to help defend your answer. Explain, too, how this rumor might have started. (Hint: Were people thinking of space and the moon as the same thing?)

The Architect's Diary

Devin's voice crackled with excitement. "Look at this!" he said. "I found a page of James Hoban's diary. Mara, this is a real find! I wonder how it got in this old box of documents."

"Who is James Hoban?" asked Mara.

"Hoban was an **architect**," answered Devin. He was born in 1758 in Ireland. He immigrated to the United States after the Revolutionary War. Hoban's the man who designed the White House for George Washington. The White House is the President's private home. The White House is the only private residence of a head of state that is open to the public, free of charge. It was Washington himself that decided our nation's capital would not be in a northern or southern state. It would be in the middle. It would be in a district by the Potomac River. It would be a planned city, built from scratch."

"The architecture of the White House is striking," Mara commented. "It is simple but elegant. If Hoban was the architect, he did a great job."

"I know Hoban was the architect. There was a competition. Nine architects sent in plans for the president's house. Washington picked Hoban as the winner. Washington liked the simple elegance of Hoban's design," said Devin. "Now take a look at what Hoban wrote in his diary."

> *August 9, 1776*
>
> *I met with George Washington today in the White House. What a feeling it was to walk up to 1600 Pennsylvania Avenue and see the finished building. The outside walls were straight and plain, but the rounded dome on top kept it from being too simple. The building site, just east of the Potomac River, was ideal.*
>
> *I told Washington that it was an honor to be his chosen architect. I told him that I had never designed such a huge building before. After all, it is not every day that one is asked to design a building that has 132 rooms, 35 bathrooms, 28 fireplaces, 412 doors, 147 windows, eight staircases, three elevators, a movie theater, and six levels!*

When Mara finished reading, she said, "Devin, this can't be real. It could not have been written by the White House architect."

"How could you know?" asked Devin. "You didn't even know who the White House architect was. I know for certain that James Hoban designed the White House. His design did include an oval office. His design even earned him a gold medal."

Why doesn't Mara think the diary is real? It is time to check facts.

Dictionary

1. What does an architect do? _____

   _____

2. Why might an architect want to know how and who will use a building before he or she designs it? _____

   _____

Search Engine/Encyclopedia

Key Words: 🔍 *White House history*   🔍 *White House facts*

1. Was James Hoban the White House architect? _____

2. Is the address of the White House 1600 Pennsylvania Ave? _____

3. Which president was the first to move into the White House, and when?

   _____

4. Has the White House changed or been added on to since it was first built?

   _____

   If your answer was "yes," describe one addition and when it happened.

   _____

5. What is listed in the story that most likely was added after the White House was built? _____

Atlas

Which direction is the White House from the Potomac River?

Ⓐ north   Ⓑ south   Ⓒ east   Ⓓ west

In Your Own Words

Write a paragraph in which you explain why someone at first might believe the diary entry was written by James Hoban. Next, explain why this cannot be so. Use as many examples from the story as you can.

Marathon Legend

"I want to tell you about Claire Lomas," Jon said to his friend Adele. "She was thrown from a horse and paralyzed from the chest down, but she just completed a marathon in England."

"I know all about marathons," Adele said. "It's an endurance race because of its length. The distance is 26.2 miles. The name comes from a legend about a Greek messenger. In the legend, the messenger is sent from the battlefield of Marathon all the way to Athens to announce that the Persians have been defeated. The runner runs the entire distance without stopping, only to collapse and die after announcing the victory.

"So," Adele continued, "Lomas must have been racing in the wheelchair division. The women's wheelchair record is close to an hour and a half. Can you imagine pushing your wheelchair 26.2 miles? To cover that distance in that time, one would have to be traveling on the average over 17 miles per hour! How fast did Lomas go?"

"It took her 17 days," answered Jon, "but she wasn't in a wheelchair. She walked."

"I don't believe you," Adele said. "You said she was paralyzed from the chest down. It would be impossible for her to walk."

"She can't walk," Jon said. "That's what makes her story all the more amazing. Lomas was the first paralyzed person to ever complete a marathon standing upright on her own two legs. She did it by wearing a borrowed robotic suit. The suit was like an exoskeleton."

"You mean her suit was like a skeleton outside of the body?" asked Adele.

"Exactly," answered Jon. "The suit weighed 18 kilograms and cost 43,000 British pounds. It was equipped with motion sensors, rechargeable batteries, and a computer system. The machine didn't walk for Lomas. Lomas controlled it with upper-body movements while balancing herself on crutches. By leaning forward, Lomas would trigger the machine to lift the legs. Then she had to maintain a constant, rhythmic motion forward. If she didn't, the machine would fall backwards into a sitting mode. Why didn't Lomas fall forward? That's when her upper body strength and the crutches came into play. Lomas used the crutches to balance herself.

"Lomas could only go about 1.5 miles a day," continued Jon. "Most people would have quit, but Lomas **persevered**. She never gave up. Day after day, she would return to the course, starting up where she had left the day before. Lomas said that several times she wanted to quit because of the terrible pain from the crutches. Despite what she suffered, she persevered and finished."

"She's like a modern-day legend!" Adele said. "Whenever people want to quit something hard, they can think about Lomas. They can be inspired by her perseverance. That will help them not give up when the going gets tough."

Is this story believable or impossible? It is time to check facts.

Dictionary

1. When one perseveres, one _____.

2. A turtle and a rabbit run a race. The turtle wins. Which animal do you think most likely persevered? Explain your answer.

_____

_____

Calculator

Adele said the women's wheelchair record for a marathon is about an hour and a half. Is she right in saying one would be averaging over 17 miles per hour?

    miles ÷ hours = 26.2 ÷ 1.5 = _____ miles per hour, so   **Yes**   **No**

Lomas went about 1.5 miles per day. If she walked eight hours a day, her average speed in miles per hour would be

   Ⓐ 0.19 mph   Ⓑ 19 mph   Ⓒ 1.9 mph   Ⓓ 9 mph

Image Search

The robotic suit Lomas used is called the ReWalk. This suit does not have a

   Ⓐ leg brace.   Ⓑ strap.   Ⓒ face guard.   Ⓓ back brace.

Metric Converter

The robotic suit weighed 18 kilograms. 18 kg = _____ pounds

Currency Converter

1. Lomas's suit cost 43,000 British pounds. That equals _____ U.S. dollars.

2. Do you think the price will be higher or lower in 20 years? Explain. _____

In Your Own Words

Think about a time when you were doing or learning how to do something very difficult for you. Describe what it was. Then tell what and/or who helped you persevere. You can write about riding a bike, learning to read, staying calm, or anything else you want.

"I am **seething**! I am so angry, I am seeing red! I am boiling mad!" Christopher threw a map down in front of his friend Zoey and said, "Look at this! I paid 25 dollars for this world map, and it's worthless!"

Zoey picked up the map and examined it closely. "What's the problem?" she asked. "You should calm down. I wouldn't be seething with anger if I bought this map."

"Nothing is correct on this map! Mexico is above the United States, and the United States is above Canada. Everyone knows Mexico is south of the United States and should be below it on a map. Everyone knows that Canada is north of the United States and should be above it on a map," Christopher said.

"Why do you say that?" asked Zoey.

"Didn't you learn the saying *Never Eat Soggy Worms* in school?" asked Christopher. "That's how you remember directions on a map. The first letters refer to the order of directions: *N* for "north," *E* for "east," *S* for "south," and *W* for "west." North always goes to the top. East is to the right, and it comes next because that's the same direction a clock hand moves. This map has Greenland at the bottom! It has India above China, and it has Sudan above Egypt! It has Spain above France!"

Zoey started to laugh. She said, "Christopher, there is nothing wrong with this map. The world is round so there is no top or bottom. It is just the convention to put north at the top. It all started with a man named Ptolemy. Ptolemy lived from 90 AD to 168 AD. He lived in Alexandria, the capital of Egypt. When Ptolemy made his map, most of the known places in his world were in the northern hemisphere. It makes sense that Ptolemy placed all the known countries in the upper right-hand corner of his flat map. It made them easier to study. Other cartographers followed Ptolemy, and today most mapmakers put north at the top. It's just the convention. It's just the way we do things, but it doesn't have to be that way."

"So as long as every country is oriented the same way, then I can make a map with north, south, east, or west at the top?" asked Christopher.

"Yes," answered Zoey, "but sometimes it is difficult to recognize a country when it is oriented in a different direction. Its shape looks completely different. For example, some people think South America looks like an ice-cream cone. Turn it over, and it doesn't resemble an ice-cream cone at all!"

"It is easy to make mistakes," Christopher said, "especially when you are looking at things from a different orientation. Now I'm wondering if I identified the countries correctly when I told you what country was above the other."

"We can check the map together," Zoey said.

"We should," Christopher said, "because even this south-oriented map may show that something you said is incorrect."

What will Christopher and Zoey find when they work together? It is time to check facts.

Thesaurus

1. Give two synonyms for *seething*. _____ _____

2. Most likely, you would seethe with anger when someone

    Ⓐ breaks your bike on purpose.   Ⓒ asks to borrow your bike.

    Ⓑ breaks your bike accidentally.   Ⓓ asks where you bought your bike.

Atlas

Find these countries on a north-oriented map. Write in **north** or **south**.

1. Greenland is toward the _____.

2. India is _____ of China.

3. Sudan is _____ of Egypt.

4. Spain is _____ of France.

Image Search

Key Words: 🔍 *upside-down map*

Find these countries on the upside-down map. Write in **north** or **south**.

1. Greenland is toward the _____.

2. India is _____ of China.

3. Sudan is _____ of Egypt.

4. Spain is _____ of France.

5. How do your answers compare to your answers in the **Atlas** section?

_____

Search Engine/Encyclopedia

1. What is the capital of Egypt? _____

2. Is it north or south of Alexandria on an upside-down map? _____

In Your Own Words

Write a paragraph in which you explain why most maps are oriented the way they are today. Then tell if you think they should stay oriented the same way today. Give at least one reason for your answer.

A Herd with Fangs

Megan began, "The person I am thinking of has a herd of 200 animals." Ms. Marble has assigned her class a research project. Ms. Marble called the project, "Mystery Jobs." Each student was to investigate an unusual **occupation**. Part of the project involved a question time. During the question time, one student gave hints about the job he or she had researched while the rest of the class tried to guess what the unusual occupation was.

As soon as Megan had given her first hint, Sam blurted out, "I know what occupation you researched! You learned about a dairy farmer. A dairy farmer could have a herd of 200 cows that he milks several times a day."

Megan said laughing, "You are partly right. The man does milk all the animals in his herd, but he is not a dairy farmer. This man's herd is not made up of cows. The animals in this man's herd have fangs."

The class fell silent while they thought about what Megan said. Then Sophie said, "I know camels, goats, cows, and yaks are raised for milk, but none of them has fangs. Are you sure this man milks his herd? Are you sure you're talking about a farmer and not a game warden?"

"Yes," said Megan, "I am sure I am talking about a real farmer. He milks each animal in his herd every few days. A lot of his animals are six feet long, and he has to be very careful when he milks them."

"Are the animals tame?" asked Ernie.

"Most definitely not!" exclaimed Megan. "The animals are kept at a constant temperature of 78 degrees Celsius. They are milked every few days, but very little is collected. A farmer may milk 20 animals and only collect 3 tablespoons of liquid."

"I don't think what you are saying is possible," Emma said.

"It's possible!" protested Megan. "I researched a farmer who milks venomous snakes. His specialty is the Eastern diamondback rattlesnake. That's the largest venomous snake in North America. The man's name is Ken Darnell, and he lives in Alabama. Even though he's handling venomous snakes, Darnell doesn't wear gloves. He says that if you use gloves, you can't feel what the snake is doing. He wants to have contact with the snake at all times. That way, if the snake moves, he feels it immediately and can adjust to it."

"What does he do with the venom?" asked Owen.

"He turns it into a freeze-dried powder," Megan answered. "Then he sells the powder to research laboratories. Scientists use the dried powder to develop drugs to treat blood clots and heart attacks. They also use it to make antivenin for those who get bitten by venomous snakes."

"What a way to occupy one's time!" exclaimed Ms. Marble. "Megan, you did a great job, but Emma was right. There is one thing that you said that just isn't possible."

A Herd with Fangs *(cont.)*

What isn't possible? It is time to check facts.

Dictionary

1. What is the meaning of *occupation*? _____

2. What type of occupation would you like to have when you are older? Explain.

_____

_____

Image Search

1. Find images of snake fangs. Draw a quick outline sketch of their shape.

2. Are the fangs on the top or bottom part of a snake's mouth? _____

Temperature Converter

1. 78 degrees Celsius = _____ degrees Fahrenheit

2. Would a snake most likely be kept at 78°C or 78°F? Explain your answer.

_____

_____

Search Engine/Encyclopedia

Write **True** or **False**. If your answer is **False**, cross out the incorrect word(s) and write the correct word(s) on the line.

_____ 1. Eastern Diamondback rattlesnakes are venomous. _____

_____ 2. Eastern Diamondback rattlesnakes are the largest venomous snakes in the U.S. _____

In Your Own Words

Think about what type of person would choose to have snake-milking as his or her occupation. Describe what traits that person should have. Describe what you think his or her farm might look like and where the snakes are kept (city, country, inside, outside, separate, together, etc.) Would you ever consider this occupation?

The Perfect Soft-Boiled Egg

Randy's grandmother said, "Let me tell you the key to making the perfect soft-boiled egg. Wait until the water is boiling. Then gently drop the egg into the water. Cook it exactly three minutes—no more, no less. Do not **alter** the cooking time. If you boil the egg for any less time, it will be too runny. If you boil it longer, it will be too hard."

Randy said, "Grandma, that's not always true. You can only say the cooking time shouldn't be altered because you live in a beach house in Florida. Sometimes the cooking time needs to be altered."

Randy's grandmother said, "Randy, I could live in a beach house in California, Idaho, or New Jersey. If I wanted a perfect soft-boiled egg, I would not alter the time by a second. I would cook it for exactly three minutes."

"Grandma, I know you can't cook a soft-boiled egg in some of those places. I also know that if you cooked an egg in Nepal on the top of Mount Everest, you'd have to alter the cooking time. You'd have to cook it for much longer. If you only cooked it for three minutes, you'd be eating a very raw egg!"

"No one is going to be cooking eggs on the top of Mount Everest," laughed Randy's grandmother, "but if you did, the cooking time would be the same. You see, water always boils at the same temperature. It boils at 212 degrees Fahrenheit. I know this because that's the same as 100 degrees Celsius."

"It may be true that 100 degrees Celsius equals 212 degrees Fahrenheit," Randy said. "Water, however, doesn't always boil at the same temperature. It depends on where you are. The boiling point of water is 100 degrees Fahrenheit at sea level. When you gain altitude, there is less air pushing down on you. The higher you go, the lower the atmospheric pressure. Water boils at a lower temperature as you gain altitude because there is less atmospheric pressure.

"Mount Everest's altitude is 29,035 feet. The mountaintop air pressure there is only about one-third of that at sea level. At that altitude, the water boils at 156 degrees Fahrenheit. I think that is equal to 69 degrees Celsius. You would have to alter your cooking time at that temperature. You would have to increase it. Instead of cooking your egg three minutes, you would have to cook it 20 minutes."

Randy's grandmother asked, "What if I lived in West Virginia, high in the Rocky Mountains?" Would I have to boil my eggs there longer than three minutes?"

Randy said, "Grandma, I don't think you can make soft-boiled eggs there at all."

"Now you're not making sense," Randy's grandmother said. "I can make soft-boiled eggs anywhere I please!"

Was it Randy or his grandmother who didn't make sense? It is time to check facts.

Thesaurus

1. Write three synonyms for *alter*. _____

2. Which action would not alter or would least alter a pair of pants?

   Ⓐ hemming the pants   Ⓒ putting the pants on

   Ⓑ adding cuffs to the pants   Ⓓ dyeing the pants

Atlas

Look at a map of the United States.

1. In which of these states could there be a beach? Circle each correct answer.

   California   **Idaho**   **New Jersey**

2. List one or two mountain ranges that run through West Virginia.

   _____

Temperature Converter

1. At sea level, water boils at 212°F, which equals _____ °C.

2. On the top of Everest, water boils at 156°F. Does that equal 69°C? _____

Calculator

When calculating the temperature at which water boils, *the temperature of boiling water decreases by 1.83°F for each 1,000 feet of altitude.*

1. Mt. McKinley (Denali), Alaska: 20,000 feet

   20,000/1000 x 1.83 = _____.

   Now subtract this number from 212°F. _____

2. Mt. Whitney, California: 14,000

   14,000/1,000 x 1.83 = _____.

   Now subtract this number from 212°F. _____

In Your Own Words

Imagine that Randy's grandmother has moved from the Florida coast to Denver, Colorado. Denver is 5,000 feet above sea level. Write a paragraph explaining to Randy's grandmother why and how she should alter the time it takes to soft-boil an egg.

"My time machine works!" Rohan's little brother Tyler said.

"I don't believe you," Rohan said.

"I knew you wouldn't," Tyler responded. "That's why I made sure to come back with proof. Look at these photographs. I took them to prove that I went back in time. The first photo is when I went back to 1513. I went to St. Augustine. That's a city in northeast Florida. It's the oldest continuously occupied European-established city and port in the continental United States."

Tyler touched the photo and said, "I didn't **linger** too long in St. Augustine. It's best to only make short, quick trips when you time-travel, otherwise people start asking too many questions. I made sure to talk with Ponce de León before leaving, though. León was the first European explorer to the area. He founded the city when his ship first landed. That way he could use it as a base. He asked me, "Quieres una naranja?""

Rohan looked at the picture where his brother was pointing. His brother was standing next to a man dressed in Spanish armor. Behind them was an orange grove. The man in Spanish armor was giving an orange to Tyler.

"You can linger over that photo later," said Tyler. "Now I want you to look at this one. This one is when I went back to the Battle of Gettysburg. This battle took place in Arizona in 1863. Fighting took place for three days in July. The battle is often described as the war's turning point, but it came at great cost. There were more people who died in this battle than any other during the war."

"What war was that?" asked Rohan.

"The Revolutionary War, of course," Tyler answered. "George Washington was one of the generals. He was fighting against General Robert E. Lee. Look closely at this picture, and you can see me standing behind Washington. Washington is meeting with Major General Meade."

Rohan looked closely at the picture. He saw his brother standing behind Washington and Meade. The two generals had serious expressions on their faces.

"I don't suppose you lingered there, either?" asked Rohan.

Tyler answered, "No one would want to linger anywhere near a battlefield during battle. I suppose if you went to a historic battlefield today, you might linger over some of the exhibits."

Rohan said, "I don't believe you ever went to these places, but I will tell you what I do believe. I believe that you used a computer to alter these photos. I also believe that you should write your time-travel stories down. You can be a science-fiction writer, maybe even a famous one."

Grinning, Tyler said, "I will let you take a ride into the future on my time machine. You can find out if you are right!"

Why didn't Rohan believe that the time machine worked? It is time to check facts.

Thesaurus

1. Write down one synonym and one antonym for *linger*.

synonym: _____   antonym: _____

2. Out of the word pairs below, which taste would you most like to have linger in your mouth? (Circle your choices)

ice cream or **peanut butter**   **lemon** or **cherry**

fried crickets or **fried rice**   **hot pepper** or **cinnamon**

Atlas

Find St. Augustine, Florida. In which part of Florida is it located?

Ⓐ northeast   Ⓑ southeast   Ⓒ northwest   Ⓓ southwest

Translator (from Spanish to English)

Quieres una naranja? _____

Search Engine/Encyclopedia

Fill in the blanks.

1. When Did Ponce de Leon land in Florida? _____

2. When was St. Augustine founded? _____

3. Did Ponce de Leon bring oranges to Florida? _____

4. Which war was the Battle of Gettysburg part of? _____

5. In which state was the battle fought? _____

6. Was Washington alive during the Battle of Gettysburg? _____

In Your Own Words

Write two short paragraphs. In the first paragraph, tell how you know Tyler was making up a story. In the second paragraph, tell where you would go if you could take a trip in a time machine. Tell why. Also write about what you might do there and who or what you might see.

Georgia, Georgia

Nina felt **apprehensive**. It was her first day at a new school, and she was very nervous. She was worried that she couldn't do things the rest of the class could. Nina sat in her desk and listened carefully as each student gave a short oral presentation on one of the United States. Nina didn't recognize many of the state names, but she found the information fascinating.

After the students were done, Mr. Tanaka, the teacher, turned to Nina. "Nina," he said, "where are you from? Are you from any of the states the students reported on?"

"No," Nina said, "I'm from Georgia."

"Georgia!" exclaimed Mr. Tanaka. "No one wrote a report on Georgia. Tell us about Georgia. Don't be apprehensive. We all know you didn't have time to prepare like the other students."

Although she was very apprehensive about speaking in front of the class, Nina was determined to try. Taking a deep breath, she stood up and said, "*Gamarjoba*." She froze as the students began to laugh, but Mr. Tanaka shushed the students and told Nina to begin again. Nodding, Nina said, "We speak Georgian in Georgia. Our alphabet has 33 letters, and there are no uppercase or lowercase letters. Our letters don't look like yours at all."

Nina began to hear giggling, but she was sure of her facts and no longer felt as apprehensive. Continuing in a strong voice, she said "Georgia is a mountainous country that is bounded by the Black Sea to the west. Russia is to the north, Turkey and Armenia to the south, and Azerbaijan is to the southeast. Its capital is Tbilisi. Some of the large carnivores that live in our forests are brown bears, wolves, and lynxes. There were Caucasian leopards, but they may all be extinct. These leopards weighed up to 60 kilograms."

When Nina sat down, the class sat in stunned silence. Then Ramon spoke up. He said, "What a great imagination you have! Did you make all that up on the spot?"

"What do you mean?" asked Nina.

Ramon said, "Georgia isn't anything like that! People who live in Georgia speak English. Georgia is bounded by the Pacific Ocean to the east. The surrounding bordering states are Alabama, Kentucky, and South Carolina. Its capital is Orlando. When it comes to large carnivores, there are also alligators and bobcats. Bobcats can weigh up to 40 pounds."

Nina laughed and said, "Now you are the one with the imagination! "

Ramon turned to Mr. Tanaka. He said, "Tell her, Mr. Tanaka. Tell her I'm right."

"Students," Mr. Tanaka said, "It seems that Nina did come from Georgia, but she didn't come from the state of Georgia. She came from the country of Georgia. The country of Georgia is at the crossroads of Western Asia and Eastern Europe. Now I don't know if all the Georgia country facts were correct," Mr. Tanaka continued, "but I do know that some of the Georgia state ones need some checking."

Nina smiled when Ramon turned to her and said, "Do you want to work together?"

Which information about Georgia is wrong? It is time to check facts.

Dictionary

1. What does *apprehensive* mean? _____

2. What might be a time when you'd feel apprehension? _____

_____

Translator (from English to Georgian)

Note: You may write your answers phonetically or in the Georgian alphabet.

1. hello _____

2. thank you _____

Atlas

1. Look up both Georgias. Fill in the blanks.

	Georgia (country)	**Georgia** (U.S. state)
Capital		
Bounding Water		
Surrounding Lands		

2. Now underline the "facts" that were correctly named in the story.

Image Search

Look at the Caucasian leopard and the bobcat. How do the tails differ? _____

_____

Metric Converter

1. Caucasian leopard = 60 kilograms = _____ pounds

2. bobcat = _____ kilograms = 40 pounds

3. Which animal weighs more? _____

In Your Own Words

Imagine you are asked to give a presentation about your state. On a separate piece of paper, write down what you might say.

Around the World

Sara said, "Henry, read this newspaper article. Do you think the author is a real person? Could the events in this story be true?"

Henry picked up the newspaper article. It had yellowed with age, but it was printed on what appeared to be the front page of a real newspaper. Henry read it carefully.

New York World   *January 26, 1890*

Around the World Record Set

Yesterday I, Nellie Bly, turned fiction into fact. Jules Verne wrote a book called <u>Around the World in Eighty Days</u>. There was no doubt that it was fiction, as no one could travel around the world in 80 days. The book made me think of a challenge. I said to my editor, "Send me around the world. I will make it in 80 days!"

Just two days after I came up with the idea, I set off from New York City. I departed at 9:40 on the morning of November 14, 1889. I brought nothing more than the dress I was wearing, a sturdy coat, and a small travel bag. I carried my money—200 English pounds, gold, and some US bills—in a bag tied around my neck.

*I took boats and trains. I traveled first to England. I also went through France, Singapore, Hong King, Japan, and China. I saved time by sailing through the Suez and Panama canals. The Suez Canal cuts through the **Isthmus** of Suez and connects the Mediterranean Sea and the Red Sea. The Panama Canal cuts through the Isthmus of Panama and connects the Atlantic and Pacific Oceans. Thanks to these watery bisections across the isthmuses, I arrived at my starting place just 72 days, 6 hours, 11 minutes, and 14 seconds after I had left! My journey of 24,899 miles set a world record for circumnavigating the globe and proved that fiction can be turned into fact."*

Henry put down the page and said, "There was a reporter who used the pen name Nellie Bly. Bly did set a time record for going around the world. How strange to think that once upon a time people thought circumnavigating the globe in 80 days was fast!

"So it's all true," Sara exclaimed. "This is a real article written by Nellie Bly."

"I didn't say that," Henry said. "I'm not so sure all the canal facts are correct."

"I'm pretty sure they are," Sara said. "I know the Suez Canal bisects the Isthmus of Suez. It does connect the Mediterranean Sea and the Red Sea. Using this canal, Bly could sail from the Red Sea directly into the Atlantic Ocean. The Panama Canal does bisect the Isthmus of Panama. Sailing through this canal saved Bly a trip around Africa. Henry, I think we may have a real copy of Bly's last report on her trip. This is really exciting!"

"I think you and I both need to investigate some things first," Henry said.

Around the World *(cont.)*

What do you think Henry wants to investigate? It is time to check facts.

Dictionary

1. What is an isthmus? _____

2. Why isn't an island an isthmus? Use a complete sentence to explain.

   _____

   _____

Currency Converter

As Bly traveled, she would need to convert her currency. 200 British pounds =

1. _____ U.S. dollars?

2. _____ Chinese yuan (CNY)

3. _____ Japanese yen (JPY)

Atlas

Find the Suez Canal and the Panama Canal. Complete the chart.

	Suez Canal	**Panama Canal**
1. Which countries are they located in?		
2. Which waterways do they connect?		
3. Which continent do they make it possible to not sail around?		

Search Engine/Encyclopedia

1. Nellie Bly's real name was _____.

2. The Suez Canal was completed in _____.

3. The Panama Canal was completed in _____.

In Your Own Words

Write a paragraph in which you briefly tell who Bly was and what she did. Then describe, in order, the bodies of water she would have to sail on during her trip. (You should list three oceans, one canal, and two seas in your answer.) In your paragraph, use sequence words like *first, second, third, in the beginning, next,* and *finally.*

Hint: Use the dates the canals were completed to help you.

Octopus in the Post Office

Jack said, "Ms. Swan, Anne is making up stories. She says that an octopus wanted to live in a post office. How can an octopus want to live in a post office?"

Ms. Swan said, "Anne, I agree with Jack. I don't think an octopus can want to live in a post office."

Anne answered, "If the post office is under the water it can! You see, someone in Vanuatu came up with an **ingenious** way to attract tourists. In 2003 they built a post office. They were very clever about where they built it. Where did they build it? They built it 50 meters off shore and 3 meters under the water!

"The post office is manned by postal workers that have been trained as divers. They don't wear regular uniforms. Instead, they wear wet suits and face masks. They breathe oxygen from tanks they carry on their backs. Bright tropical fish live in the post office. They did have a problem with an octopus that wanted to live in it, too. Fortunately, they were able to coax the octopus out and into a nearby rock crevice.

"The post office has proved to be an ingenious way to make money. That's because it has become very popular among tourists. Over 100,000 tourists have bought special waterproof postcards and posted them at the post office. The cards are cancelled underwater with a special seal. Cruise ships now make special stops so people on board can get off and swim to the post office. The tourists enjoy having to wear swimsuits and breathe through snorkels while they mail a card."

Ms. Swan laughed and said, "The post office under the water was indeed an ingenious idea! The person who thought it up was very clever. I'd like to visit that post office some day. I would enjoy seeing colorful fish swim by me as I waited in line. I wouldn't want to see an octopus though! That would scare me!"

Jack still wasn't convinced. "I've never heard of Vanuatu before. Where is it exactly?"

"It's a real country," Anne assured Jack. "It's an island nation in the South Pacific Ocean. It is east of northern Australia and west of Fiji. It became an independent nation on July 30, 1980."

Jack walked over to a map on the wall. The map was very old.

"Anne," Jack said, "you tell a good story, but look on this map. Vanuatu is not where you say it is. There is only a place called the New Hebrides. Are you sure you're not making up a story?"

Is Vanuatu a real place? It is time to check facts.

Thesaurus

1. Write down two synonyms for the word *ingenious*. _____

   _____

2. Think of an invention that you feel is ingenious. Explain your choice.

   why you think it was or is ingenious. _____

   _____

Image Search

Key Words: 🔍 *underwater post office Vanuatu*

Would there be room for both the octopus and the postal worker in the post office?

Explain your answer. _____

_____

Metric Converter

Where was the post office built?

1. 50 meters from shore = _____ feet

2. 3 meters under the water = _____ feet

Atlas

1. Is Vanuatu an island nation in the South Pacific Ocean? _____

2. Is it east of northern Australia and west of Fiji? _____

Search Engine/Encyclopedia

1. Was Vanuatu once called the New Hebrides? _____

In Your Own Words

Write a paragraph explaining why Jack might have a hard time believing Anne. In your paragraph, tell why it did not help that Jack looked at a very old map. Conclude your paragraph by describing how you might have reacted if you were Jack.

Organs You Can't Play

Marshall said, "I am done studying for my exam. I know everything I need to know about the organs I will be tested on. May I go play now?"

Marshall's younger brother Jonathon said, "We don't have an organ for you to play."

Marshall's older brother Hugh said to Jonathon, "Marshall doesn't mean the musical instrument organ. He means the parts of the body that perform a specific function." Then Hugh turned to Marshall and said, "Why don't you tell Jonathon which organs you studied?"

"The first organ I studied was one of the **vital** organs," Marshall explained. "Vital organs are the ones that are absolutely necessary. I studied the heart. The heart is a muscular pump that is located just left-of-center in the chest. This vital organ is about as big as your fist, and it will continue to grow, just as you do. The bigger you are, the bigger your heart. Your heart powers oxygen-rich blood around your body to feed your body cells. Every time your heart pushes out blood and then relaxes is a heartbeat."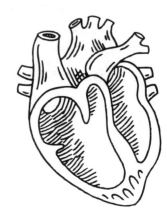

"How many times does my heart beat?" asked Jonathon.

"The average heartbeat is 72 times a minute," answered Marshall. "That means in the course of the day, it beats 7,200 times. That means in one year, it beats 1 million times!"

"If my heart works that hard, then it must be the biggest organ in my body," Jonathon said.

"Correct," Marshall said. "The heart is the biggest organ in your body. Now can you tell me what some other organs are?"

Jonathon asked, "Are the lungs and the liver vital organs?"

"Very good," answered Marshall. "People have two lungs and two livers. The lungs deliver oxygen from the air to your bloodstream when you breathe in. They also release waste carbon dioxide from the blood when you breathe out. Livers do several things. They process some nutrients and store others. They remove harmful substances from the blood, and they recycle worn-out red blood cells. Your two livers are located below your intestines."

Hugh interrupted and said, "There is one vital organ you forgot. It's the one that collects, interprets, and sends out information through the nervous system. In adults, this vital organ weighs about three pounds. There are about 400 miles of blood vessels in it. What vital organ is this? It's your brain! Other animals may have larger brains than you, but you have the largest brain to body size. Now it is time for both of you to use your big brains and figure out what facts I heard you discussing that you got mixed up on. Marshall, this is absolutely vital if you want to do well on the exam."

Organs You Can't Play (cont.)

What did Marshall and Jonathon get mixed up? It is time to check facts.

Thesaurus

1. What are two synonyms for *vital*? _____ _____

2. You are going to play baseball. Name three vital pieces of equipment.

_____ _____ _____

Calculator

Check Marshall's math to find how many heartbeats a person might have in a day, a year, and by the age of 70.

1.
    __72__ times a minute
    _____ minutes in an hour
x _____ hours in a day
_____
= _____ heartbeat in a day

2.
    _____ heartbeats in a day
x __365__ days in a year
_____
= _____ heartbeats per year

3. Were Marshall's numbers too low or too high? _____

Search Engine/Encyclopedia

Write **True** or **False**. If your answer is **False**, cross out the incorrect word(s) and write the correct word(s) on the line.

_____ **1.** The heart is the biggest organ. _____

_____ **2.** People have two lungs. _____

_____ **3.** People have two livers. _____

Image Search

Find a diagram of the body organs. Marshall said . . .

    "The heart is located just left-of-center in the chest."

    "Your two livers are located below your intestines."

Which organ did Marshall locate correctly? _____

In Your Own Words

About how many times has your heart beat in your lifetime? Think about how you would calculate the answer. Then, using words and numbers, show how you got your answer. You may write your answer in paragraph form, or you can break it down into numbered steps.

The Greatest Inventor

"Garrett Augustus Morgan is the greatest inventor," Lily said.

"Thomas Alva Edison is the greatest inventor," Blake said.

Lily and Blake went to Ms. Finch, their teacher. "Who is right?" they asked.

Ms. Finch said, "I will listen to both of you. Then I will tell you what I think."

Lily said, "Morgan was born in Paris, France, in 1877. He came to the United States and lived in Kentucky and Ohio. While he was in Ohio, he invented a Safety Hood. He got a **patent** for his invention in 1914."

"Do you know what a patent is for?" interrupted Ms. Finch.

"A patent is like a license," Lily answered. "You apply for it in a government patent office. If granted, it gives you the sole right to make, use, or sell your invention for so many years."

"As I was saying," Lily continued, "Morgan got his patent, but no one would buy his Safety Hood. Then on July 14, 1916, something terrible happened. There was an explosion in a tunnel. The tunnel was 250 feet below Lake Erie. The tunnel filled with smoke and poisonous gas. Workers got trapped. Firefighters came to rescue them, but they couldn't. Several firefighters died. Then Morgan and his brother came. They didn't care that the tunnel was under the biggest of the Great Lakes. They went right in and saved 32 workers. How did they do it? They wore Morgan's patented Safety Hoods! After the news spread about what Morgan had done, fire departments all over the country bought Morgan's invention. Today we know it as a gas mask. Morgan died in 1963."

"My turn," Blake said. "Edison was born in 1847. He was born in Milan, Italy. He came to the United States and lived in Ohio and New Jersey. Edison was granted over 1,000 patents. He got a patent for a light bulb in 1880. He gave us things like the phonograph and a car battery. He liked to say, 'Genius is 1 percent inspiration and 99 percent perspiration.' My favorite thing he said was, 'I have not failed. I've just found 10,000 ways that won't work.' Edison died in 1931."

Thomas Alva Edison

"That means Edison had many more years than Morgan to invent things," Lily said.

Ms. Finch said, "Unfortunately, I can't say which man was the greatest inventor. I think they were both great. Fortunately, I can't say that I found 10,000 things wrong with all that you said. I only found four. Can you figure out what?"

Lily started to laugh. She asked Blake, "Do you think we are going to work up a sweat while we figure this out?"

Which four things do Lily and Blake need to figure out? It is time to check facts.

Dictionary

1. What is the meaning of the word *patent?* _____

_____

2. Does your meaning mostly agree with what Lily said?　　**Yes**　　**No**

Image Search

Key Words:　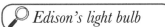　

Think about what light bulbs and gas masks look like today. Which item do you think has changed the most? Give your opinion in one or two sentences.

_____

_____

_____

Search Engine/Encyclopedia

Write **True** or **False**. If your answer is **False**, cross out the incorrect word(s) and write the correct word(s) on the line.

_____ **1.** Garrett Augustus Morgan was born in Paris, France. _____

_____ **2.** Thomas Alva Edison was born in Milan, Italy. _____

_____ **3.** The largest Great Lake is Lake Erie. _____

Calculator

About how many years did each inventor live?

1. Morgan = 1877–1963 = _____ years

2. Edison = 1847–1931 = _____ years

3. Who lived longer? _____

In Your Own Words

Write one or two paragraphs in which you describe how your life and the world might be different if there were no light bulbs or gas masks.

Or, write a paragraph with a surprise ending. Someone thinks they are going to Paris or Milan, and they end up being in a very different place than they expected!

Where Are the Strawberries?

Emma lived in San Francisco. Emma liked living in an urban environment. She liked the big and bustling city with all of its streets, buildings, and people. She liked all the things there were to do. Whenever Emma would go to the store with her mother, Emma would think, "Everything is **available** here! There is nothing one can't buy!"

Then one day Emma found out not everything was available. There were no strawberries in the city. Not one of the red, pretty berries that Emma loved to eat were anywhere to be found. The store manager told Emma, "We will get some more in a week or so. If you want some right now, you will have to go to Watsonville. They are available at a farm there, but you will have to pick your own."

Emma asked her mother, "Mom, will you please take me to Watsonville? I really want some strawberries. There is a farm in Watsonville where they are available if you pick your own. I looked at the map, and it's not that far. Watsonville is less than 90 miles north of San Francisco. To get there, we can drive along the coast of the Pacific Ocean."

Emma continued, "I didn't know this, but I found this out when I was looking up strawberry farms in Watsonville. California is the nation's leading producer of strawberries. A big reason is that its western ocean exposure provides moderate temperatures year round. The monthly average high temperature in Watsonville ranges from 16 to 23 degrees Fahrenheit. The monthly average low temperature ranges from 4 to 12 degrees. The warm sunny days and cool foggy nights are the perfect combination for growing the perfect berries.

"I'm getting hungry just thinking about all the berries I can pick," Emma said. "Oh, I almost forgot," Emma said, continuing with excitement, "the best thing is that there are a lot more than strawberry trees on this farm. There are also broccoli, artichoke, and carrot trees! All of those fruits are available for the picking, too!" Suddenly Emma stopped talking. With a worried look on her face, she asked, "Do you think they provide us with a ladder, or do we have to bring our own?"

Emma's mother started to laugh. She said, "I am going to drive you to Watsonville right now. Some of the things you have said have shown me you need to spend some time out of the city. You need to spend time in the country."

Where Are the Strawberries? *(cont.)*

Why did Emma's mother think she needs to spend time out of the city? It is time to check facts.

Dictionary

1. When something is available, it _____.

2. If refreshments are available,

    Ⓐ one cannot eat.   Ⓒ one can eat now.

    Ⓑ one must eat later.   Ⓓ one must take food home.

Atlas

Key Words: 🔍 *driving distance from San Francisco to Watsonville*

1. Do you drive north or south when you go to Watsonville? _____

2. About how many miles away is it? _____

Temperature Converter

1. Average monthly high: 16–23° Celsius = _____ ° Fahrenheit

2. Average monthly low: 4–12° Celsius = _____ ° Fahrenheit

3. Did Emma use degrees Celsius or Fahrenheit? _____

4. Which one do you think she meant to say and why? _____

Image Search

Look up strawberry plants, broccoli plants, artichoke plants, and carrot plants.

1. Would you describe any as trees? _____

2. Would you need to use a ladder to pick any of them? _____

Search Engine/Encyclopedia

Classify each of the following as a fruit or a vegetable.

1. strawberry _____   **3.** broccoli _____

2. artichoke _____   **4.** carrot _____

In Your Own Words

Write a paragraph in which you describe what type of environment you live in.
Describe what kinds of things are available to buy, see, or do. Then tell one or two
things that you wish were available but are not available where you live.

Eggs, Tears, and the Nile

Noor went to visit her grandfather. He had just come back from a trip sailing down the Nile River. Noor's grandfather was getting frail. He couldn't do anything too **strenuous**. A river tour was a way he could see new things without having to do strenuous activity. Now that he was back, Noor's grandfather wanted to show Noor pictures and tell her about his trip. Noor knew he wanted help with something, too. Noor thought he might need help with something too strenuous for him—perhaps lifting something heavy.

When Noor got there, her grandfather immediately gave her a photo. "This is a picture of a Nile crocodile," he said. "These are amazing mammals. Did you know that when the female lays her eggs, it's neither male nor female? It's the average temperature during the middle third of their incubation period that determines the sex! Our nature guide told us if the temperature of the nest is below 31.7 degrees Celsius or above 34.5 degrees Celsius, it is a female."

"You just taught me something new, Grandpa," Noor said.

"I'll bet you don't know about crocodile tears. Can I teach you about them?"

"Yes, please," answered Noor, sitting back in her chair.

"There is an expression about crocodile tears," Noor's grandfather said. "If you shed 'crocodile tears', people think you are faking it. You are not really crying or sad. That's because crocodiles shed tears while they are eating their victims, but the crocodiles aren't really crying. Crocodiles don't feel bad about their victims. They shed tears because they swallow large lumps of meat. To swallow, their jaw muscles have to move strenuously, expanding and contracting. The pressure created by the moving muscles squeezes tears out of the crocodile's eyes."

Noor said, "I didn't know that! I always wondered where the expression 'crying crocodile tears' came from, and now I know!"

"I'll tell you more," Noor's grandfather said. "The Nile River is the longest river in the world. The guide said that the length of the river runs northward through 10 countries. The White Nile and the Blue Nile are its two major tributaries. The Nile's source is the Mediterranean Sea. That's where we started when we set sail in Egypt."

"Did you sail through any of the other countries?" asked Noor.

"Only Uganda," Noor's grandfather answered. "That's the country immediately south of Egypt. Then we had to turn around."

Noor said, "That must have been quite a trip, Grandpa. Now what strenuous activity did you want me to help you with? What needs lifting?"

Noor's grandfather started to laugh. He said, "I just need some strenuous brain work! Tell me, how long is the Nile River in miles and how many degrees Fahrenheit does a crocodile nest have to be to get males? I'm straight on everything our guide told us, but I always get mixed up when I convert Celsius to Fahrenheit."

"Grandpa, you're mixed up on three things," Noor said gently. "Don't worry. I'll help you get everything straight. I'll convert the metric measurements into standard, too."

Eggs, Tears, and the Nile *(cont.)*

Which three things has Noor's grandfather gotten mixed up? It is time to check facts.

Dictionary

1. What does *strenuous* mean? _____

_____

2. Which would you find more strenuous: running around the block or swimming half that distance? Answer in a complete sentence.

_____

_____

Temperature Converter

Female crocodiles develop in eggs that are . . .

1. below 31.7 degrees Celsius, which equals _____ ° Fahrenheit.

2. above 34.5 degrees Celsius, which equals _____ ° Fahrenheit.

Atlas

Could someone sail south from Egypt immediately into Uganda? _____

If not, which country or countries is or are in between? _____

_____

Search Engine/Encyclopedia

Write **True** or **False**. If your answer is **False**, cross out the incorrect word(s) and write the correct word(s) on the line.

_____ **1.** Crocodiles are mammals. _____

_____ **2.** The Mediterranean Sea is the source of the Nile. _____

_____ **3.** The two major tributaries of the Nile are the White Nile and the Blue Nile. _____

In Your Own Words

Write a paragraph or two in which you explain the phrase "crocodile tears." Tell what it means and how it might have started. Then briefly describe a time when you or someone else has shed crocodile tears. (If you want, you can make one up. If you do make one up, you can be serious or silly.)

Enough Rice?

"I really dislike fairy tales," Jennifer said. "Fairy tales can't teach you anything."

"I know a fairy tale that teaches you to think ahead," Alexander said. "The story comes from India, and it deals with an **astronomical** number and the game of chess."

"I don't care about really large numbers or the game of chess," Jennifer said. "Chess is just a game that uses a board with 64 squares. There are eight across and eight down, and the squares alternate in color. There are two players. Each opponent has a king, a queen, two rooks, two bishops, two knights, and eight pawns. Each player tries to take their opponent's king. You warn your opponent that their king is in danger of being taken by saying, 'Check.' When your opponent's king can't escape, you say 'Checkmate.'"

Alexander said, "You may know about chess, but now you can find out about the astronomical number. Listen carefully." Alexander began,

> Long ago in ancient India, a wise man brought a new game to the emperor. The game was what we now know as chess. The wise man told the emperor that it was a game of strategy and skill. It was a game where the player had to think carefully before every move.
>
> The emperor was so pleased with the game that he told the wise man he could have anything he wanted. The wise man said he didn't need anything, but the emperor insisted. Finally, to teach the emperor a lesson, the wise man said, "If you really want to give me anything, you can give me one grain of rice for the first square of the game board. The next day, give me two grains of rice on the second square. Every day, until all the squares are filled, double the amount of rice on each square."
>
> "Why, that's nothing," the emperor cried, "There are only 64 squares! You will only get rice for 64 days. I have a huge kingdom with large rice fields. What a silly man to ask for so little. I would have given you so much more."
>
> The next day, the wise man was given one grain of rice. The day after, he was given two grains of rice. But well before the 64 days were up, it was the emperor who was shown to be the silly man. The emperor should have thought carefully before he made his promise.

When Alexander stopped speaking, Jennifer said, "That's the end of the tale? There's nothing in it about an astronomical number. This story makes no sense at all."

Alexander said, "The lesson is that the emperor should have thought ahead. He should have calculated the number of rice grains he needed. If he had, he would have known that the amount of rice he needed was astronomical. The amount was so large that every grain of rice in his kingdom was not enough."

Jennifer said, "There were only 64 squares, so of course he had enough rice! Here, I'll prove it to you with pennies."

Alexander said, "Are you sure you don't want to think ahead?"

Enough Rice? *(cont.)*

Can Jennifer prove that the emperor had enough rice? It is time to check facts.

Thesaurus

1. Write three synonyms for *astronomical.* _____

_____   _____

2. Which is there an astronomical number of?

    Ⓐ continents   Ⓑ oceans   Ⓒ spaceships   Ⓓ stars

Image Search

Find a chessboard. The story describes it in this way: "There are eight across and eight down, and the squares alternate in color." Is this true?   **Yes**   **No**

If it's not true, what is wrong? _____

Calculator

Use a calculator to double the amounts. (Multiply each number on the square by 2 for the next square.)

Square 1: _1_   Square 8: _____   Square 15: _____

Square 2: _2_   Square 9: _____   Square 16: _____

Square 3: _4_   Square 10: _____   Square 17: _____

Square 4: ___   Square 11: _____   Square 18: _____

Square 5: ___   Square 12: _____   Square 19: _____

Square 6: ___   Square 13: _____   Square 20: _____

Square 7: ___   Square 14: _____   Square 64 = <u>9,223,372,036,854,775,808</u>

For a real challenge, you may go all the way up to 64 and then add up all the numbers!

*The total number of rice grains would make a pile of rice larger than Mount Everest!

In Your Own Words

Write a paragraph in which you tell about a time when you (or someone you know) should have thought about what you said or promised before you said or promised it.

Or, summarize a fairy tale you like and a lesson it might teach you.

"I really am uncomfortable around spiders," Ms. Carter said. "In fact, they **petrify** me. I see a spider, and I become so scared that I can't move. Although I am petrified of spiders, I like reading about them in legends and stories. There is one wonderful ancient Greek story about the woman the Greeks believed to be the ancestor of all spiders. The woman's name was Arachne. Arachne was a talented weaver whose weavings were considered to be the most beautiful in all of Greece. The problem was that this made her too proud. Arachne became so proud that she began to show off and tell everyone that even the goddess Athena wasn't as good a weaver as she. Athena became so angry at this that she turned Arachne into a spider! Arachne could no longer weave beautiful cloth, but she could weave a web."

"Hey," said Ben, "I bet spiders got the name *arachnids* from that myth. Many people think spiders are insects, but spiders aren't insects at all. They are arachnids."

"Are you afraid of spiders, Ben?" asked Ms. Carter.

"I don't have arachnophobia, so no, they don't petrify me," Ben answered. "In fact, I think spiders are one of nature's most wonderful marvels. Take the bolas spider, for example. This spider doesn't use its silk to make a web. Instead, it spins a ball of sticky silk on the end of a strong silk strand. Then, when a moth flies near, the bolas spider swings the sticky ball at the moth! If it hits it, the moth sticks to the ball, and the spider reels it in! Other spiders, like jumping spiders, leap onto their prey. Did you know that jumping spiders can leap 50 times their body length?"

Suddenly Ronnie cried, "Ms. Carter, don't move! There's a spider crawling up your pants leg!"

Ms. Carter was petrified. Her face turned white, and she remained as still as a stone.

Ben came closer and said, "Ms. Carter, it's not a spider, so you shouldn't be scared."

"Yes, it is," Ronnie insisted. "See, it has six legs and three body parts." Pretty soon all the children in the class were around Ms. Carter and looking at the creature on her leg. They all began to argue about the creature being a spider or not.

Finally, Ms. Carter could take it no longer. She reached down, brushed the creature off of her pants, grabbed a clear plastic cup from her desk, and trapped the creature under it. Just then Carlos came in holding a cardboard shoebox. "Oh, good!" he said happily, "You caught Reina a cricket."

"Who is Reina?" asked Ms. Carpenter.

"My pet tarantula," answered Carlos as he lifted the lid off the shoebox. "Ms. Carter, do you want to hold her?"

"No, I don't," Ms. Carter said firmly, "but I think everyone needs to count your queen's legs and body parts."

Why should the class count the queen's legs and body parts? It is time to check facts.

Dictionary

1. What do you do when you are petrified? _____

2. Most likely, if wood has become petrified, it

Ⓐ is part of a living tree.   Ⓑ has become fossilized.

Image Search

Key Words: 🔍 *spider body parts*

1. Draw a basic spider with the correct number of legs and body parts. Label these parts: *cephalothorax, abdomen, legs.*

2. Find a picture of a *bolas spider*. Is its abdomen large or small? _____

Calculator

1. A jumping spider can jump 50 times its body length.

Multiply your height by 50: _____ x 50 = _____

Circle **Yes** or **No**. If you could jump like a jumping spider, could you jump as far as a . . .

2. basketball court (94 feet) **Yes   No**   **4.** school bus (40 feet)   **Yes   No**

3. football field (360 feet) **Yes   No**   **5.** minivan (16 feet)   **Yes   No**

Translator (from Spanish to English)

1. *Reina* _____

2. If Carlos got a male tarantula and wanted its name to match Reina's, which name would he most likely pick?

Ⓐ Rojo   Ⓑ Ruina   Ⓒ Reciente   Ⓓ Rey

In Your Own Words

How do you feel about spiders? Write a paragraph in which you describe your feelings and why. Give an example of an experience or observation you have had with a spider. When you write, use the word *petrify* or *petrified* at least once. (You may put the word *not* in front of *petrified* if you want!)

A Day Longer than a Year

"I am ten years old," said Carly. "A year is the time it takes a planet to make one **revolution** around the sun. So going around the sun one single time takes Earth 365.24 days. To make things easier, we say one year is 365 days. Then every four years, we have a leap year. On leap years, February has 29 days instead of 28 days."

Greg said, "A day is the length of time that it takes a planet to rotate, or spin, on its axis. It takes Earth almost 24 hours to spin completely around. To make things easier, we just say one day on Earth is 24 hours."

"Let's see," said Carly, "if I am 10 years old, then that means that during my lifetime, Earth has made 10 revolutions around the sun. It means that I am 3,652.4 days old because Earth has rotated on its axis that many times. Wow, I sound a lot older if I say how many days I am."

"You wouldn't sound older on Venus," Greg said. "On Venus, a day is longer than a year."

"That's impossible," Carly said laughing. "A day can't be longer than a year."

"Yes, it can," said Greg. "Venus is the second planet from the sun. It is the brightest natural object in the sky after the moon. And like the moon, it can even cast shadows!"

"That's interesting," said Carly, "but that doesn't explain how I can be a greater number of days old than years old."

Greg said, "Venus is the planet with the longest day. One day on Venus is equal to 243 Earth days. That's because it takes Venus 243 Earth days to spin completely around on its axis. A year on Venus is only 224.7 Earth days. That's because it takes Venus 224.7 Earth days to make a complete revolution around the sun. Since it takes Venus longer to spin around on its axis than it takes to go around the sun, its day is longer than its year."

"What about Jupiter?" asked Carly. "Am I more days old than years old on Jupiter?"

"Definitely not!" answered Greg. "Jupiter is the largest planet and fifth from the sun. It has the shortest day out of all the planets. A day on Jupiter is only 9.8 Earth hours long! When astronomers look at Jupiter from Earth, they can see some of its features change! A year on Jupiter is 11.86 Earth years because that is how long it takes for Jupiter to make one complete revolution around the Sun."

"So if I lived on Venus, I'd be 15 days old, but I would be 16.2 years old. How old would I be if I lived on Jupiter?"

Greg began to laugh. He said, "You would be almost 9,000 days old, but you wouldn't even be one year old! You'd still be waiting for a birthday cake with one candle!"

A Day Longer than a Year *(cont.)*

Would Carly still be waiting for a birthday on Jupiter? It is time to check facts.

Thesaurus

1. Which word is not a synonym for *revolution* the way it is used in this story?

Ⓐ turn   Ⓑ spin   Ⓒ rotation   Ⓓ still

Image Search

1. Is Venus the 2nd planet from the sun and Jupiter the 5th? **Yes** **No**

2. Which planet is 3rd? _____ Which is 4th? _____

Calculator

Use a calculator to find out your age in days and years for each planet.

Step 1: Multiply your age in years by 365. _____ x 365 = _____ days old

Step 2: Divide your day number by each planet's **rotation period**.

Planet	Rotation Period	Your Age in Days on Each Planet
Mercury	58.6 days	
Venus	243 days	
Mars	1.03 days	
Jupiter	.41 days	
Saturn	.45 days	
Uranus	.72 days	
Neptune	.67 days	

Step 3: Divide your day number (for Mercury and Venus) or your year number (for the other planets) by each planet's **revolution period**.

Planet	Rotation Period	Your Age in Years on Each Planet
Mercury	88 days	
Venus	224.7 days	
Mars	1.9 years	
Jupiter	11.96 years	
Saturn	29.5 years	
Uranus	84.0 years	
Neptune	164.8 years	

In Your Own Words

Imagine how people might celebrate birthdays on Jupiter. Are birthdays more special because they don't happen very often? Is there a party, gifts, or games? Explain.

Seaworthy Sale?

Mark and his father walked along the marina until they found the boat with the "For Sale" sign on it. They studied the **vessel** in the water until a man came up from the boat's cabin and invited them on. "Come aboard and take a look," he said. "I'll show you around."

As Mark and his father stepped onto the front of the boat, the man said, "Since you got on at the front, we will start our tour here at the stern."

"Is the front of a boat the stern?" asked Mark's father.

"Yes," said the man. "The stern is always the front or forward part of any sailing vessel and the bow is the back. Port is the left side of the boat when looking forward, and starboard is the right side of the boat when looking forward."

"So where has he sailed?" asked Mark's father.

"Oh, you mean, 'Where has *she* sailed,'" the man said. "All boats are referred to as *she*. And the answer is that I just took her on an expedition to the world's largest island: Madagascar."

"Is Madagascar the big island off of the southeastern coast of Africa?" asked Mark's father.

"That's the one," answered the man. "It lies in the Indian Ocean, and I always like sailing those waters because the Indian Ocean is the warmest ocean."

The man continued, "However, sailing through the warmest ocean was only a bonus. I chose Madagascar as my destination because of the animals. Madagascar is a hotspot of biodiversity. The island is home to a vast array of plants and animals that are found nowhere else on Earth!"

"So, why are you selling the boat? Is she still seaworthy?" asked Mark's father.

"Oh, she's a seaworthy vessel, all right," the man assured Mark's father. "It's just that I've been offered a captain's job on an ocean tanker, so I won't have time to go on any exploring expeditions. I can sell this to you at a real bargain, but you'll have to put a down payment now. Otherwise, I might sell it to a woman who is coming to look at it in the next hour."

Mark whispered to his dad, "I don't think you should put any money down, not even one Malagasy ariary. There's something very suspicious about this seller."

What is it that makes Mark suspicious? It is time to check facts.

Thesaurus

1. Write down two synonyms for the word *vessel* as it was used in this story.

_____   _____

2. Now write down two synonyms for the word *vessel* as it is used in this sentence: "I filled my drinking vessel with cool water."

_____   _____

Atlas

Write **True** or **False**. If your answer is **False**, cross out the incorrect word(s) and write the correct word(s) on the line.

1. Madagascar is located in the Indian Ocean. _____

2. Madagascar is off the southeast coast of Africa. _____

Currency Exchange

The Malagasy ariary (MGA) is the official currency of Madagascar. What is . . .

1. 1 MGA = _____ US dollars

2. 5000 MGA = _____ US dollars

Search Engine/Encyclopedia

1. Which rank is Madagascar when it comes to biggest island size?
Circle one: **1st**   **2nd**   **3rd**   **4th**   **5th**

2. Which ocean is the warmest?
Circle one: **Atlantic**   **Indian**   **Pacific**

3. Draw lines to match these terms to their correct locations on a boat.

Bow	**Back**
Stern	**Right**
Port	**Left**
Starboard	**Front**

In Your Own Words

Write a paragraph where you have Mark explain why his father should not trust the man selling the boat. Also include some reasons why someone might trust him.

Fact Find #1: Cook's Letter

Dictionary:

1. Possible answers include *easily broken* and *frail.*
2. B

Images: "Pacific," "Indian," and "Atlantic" should be circled.

Search Engine/Encyclopedia:

1. 1728–1779
2. Vitamin C
3. Scottish naval surgeon who found that a nutrient (now known to be vitamin C) in citrus foods prevented scurvy
4. oranges, lemons, limes, grapefruit, tangerines

Currency Converter: Answers depend on the current exchange rate.

Fact Find #2: Visitor from Colombia

Thesaurus:

1. Possible answers include *idle, lazy, slow,* and *sluggish.*
2. D

Metric Converter:

1. B
2. D

Translator:

1. Good morning, boys and girls.
2. two mammals

Atlas:

1. False. It is near the top of the continent.
2. True

Images: markings around eyes are like spectacles

Fact Find #3: Da Vinci and the Painting

Dictionary:

1. a person who acts as a guide or teacher, often in a museum
2. C

Images: The student sketch should show a woman with closed lips. Her teeth should not be showing.

Translator:

1. You are a child.
2. Accept appropriate responses.

Search Engine/Encyclopedia:

1. Yes
2. 1452–1519
3. Yes
4. South America
5. No

Fact Find #4: Safari Guide

Dictionary:

1. A
2. dark, unreflective clothes

Translator:

1. Freedom and Unity
2. trip

Temperature Converter:

1. 73.4°F
2. 89.6°F
3. 59°F

Search Engine/ Encyclopedia:

1. True
2. False, ~~Africa~~, Asia
3. False, ~~horizontal~~, vertical
4. False, ~~Africa~~, Asia

Currency Converter: Answers depend on the current exchange rate.

Fact Find #5: Wave-Riding Whales

Thesaurus:

1. Possible answers include *accomplishment, triumph, act,* and *adventure.*
2. Accept appropriate responses.

Atlas:

1. False, ~~Pacific~~, Atlantic
2. True
3. False, ~~north~~, south

Images: black and white

Translator:

1. black and white whales
2. Yes

Metric Converter:

1. 15,985 pounds
2. 16,000 pounds

Fact Find #6: Spaghetti Harvest

Thesaurus:

1. Possible answers include *confirm*, *validate*, *check*, and *authenticate*.
2. B

Images: It's hanging in single strands.

Search Engine/Encyclopedia:

1. United Kingdom of Great Britain and Northern Ireland
2. UK
3. Great Britain
4. United Kingdom

Translator:

Answers may depend on site chosen.

1. April Fish's
2. April Fish
3. fish
4. fish

Fact Find #7: The Ball and the Tsunami

Thesaurus:

1. Possible answers include *intelligible*, *neat*, *plain*, and *readable*.

Metric Converter:

1. 4,828
2. Yes

Calculator:

1. 7.7 miles, 12.4 kilometers
2. No

Atlas:

1. Pacific
2. No

Search Engine/Encyclopedia:

1. earthquake in Japan
2. 8.9 or 9.0 (depending on source)

Fact Find #8: Probably True, or Must Be True?

Dictionary:

1. a rope or chain, or the act of tying with a kind of rope to restrict movement
2. answers will vary

Images:

1. No
2. Yes; Accept appropriate responses.

Calculator: 1.5 hours

Metric Converter: 3,951 miles

Search Engine/Encyclopedia:

1. A
2. 238,900 miles (384,400 km)

Fact Find #9: The Architect's Diary

Dictionary:

1. An architect is someone whose job is to design buildings.
2. The answer will determine size, what kind of rooms, etc.

Search Engine/Encyclopedia:

1. Yes
2. Yes
3. John Adams, 1800
4. Yes; Answers will vary.
5. elevators, movie theater, bathrooms, some of the levels

Atlas: C

Fact Find #10: Marathon Legend

Dictionary:

1. continues in a course of action even in the face of difficulty or with little sign of success (doesn't give up)
2. The turtle most likely persevered because it is slower and would not be expected to win. So the turtle must have never stopped moving.

Calculator:

1. 17.47, Yes
2. A

Images: C

Metric Converter: 39.68 pounds

Currency Converter: Answers depend on the current exchange rate.

Fact Find #11: Upside-Down World

Thesaurus:

1. Possible answers include *furious*, *angry*, and *boiling*.
2. A

Atlas:

1. north
2.–4. south

Images:
1. south
2.–4. north
5. They are the opposite.

Search Engine/Encyclopedia:
1. Cairo
2. north

Fact Find #12: A Herd with Fangs
Dictionary:
1. a job or profession, a way of spending time
2. Accept appropriate responses.

Images:
1. Check drawings for accuracy.
2. top

Temperature Converter:
1. 172.4
2. It would have to be Fahrenheit, otherwise the snake would not survive such high temperatures.

Search Engine/Encyclopedia:
1. True
2. True

Fact Find #13: The Perfect Soft-Boiled Egg
Thesaurus:
1. Possible answers include *adapt*, *change*, and *modify*.
2. C

Atlas:
1. California, New Jersey
2. Appalachian, Allegheny

Temperature Converter:
1. 100°C
2. Yes

Calculator:
1. 36.6, 175.4°F
2. 25.62, 186.4°F

Fact Find #14: Time Machine
Thesaurus:
1. Possible synonyms include *delay*, *loiter*, *amble*, *dillydally*, and *crawl*. Possible antonyms include *go*, *hurry*, *leave*, and *rush*.
2. Answers will vary.

Atlas: A

Translator: "Do you want an orange?" Or, "Want an orange?"

Search Engine/Encyclopedia:
1. 1513
2. 1565
3. Yes
4. War Between the States, or American Civil War
5. Pennsylvania
6. No

Fact Find #15: Georgia, Georgia
Dictionary:
1. Possible answers include *anxious* or *fearful that something bad or unpleasant will happen*.

Translator: (Note: Answers are given phonetically.)
1. gamarjoba
2. didi maloba

Atlas:

Georgia (country): <u>Tbilisi</u>; <u>Black Sea</u>; <u>Russia</u>, <u>Turkey</u>, <u>Armenia</u>, <u>Azerbaijan</u>

Georgia (U.S. state): Atlanta; Atlantic Ocean; Florida, <u>Alabama</u>, Tennessee, North Carolina, <u>South Carolina</u>

Images: The bobcat's tail is shorter.

Metric Converter:
1. leopard = 132 pounds
2. bobcat = 18 kilograms
3. The leopard weighs more.

Fact Find #16: Around the World
Dictionary:
1. a narrow strip of land with water on either side, forming a link between two larger areas of land
2. An island is completely surrounded by water.

Currency Converter: Answers depend on the current exchange rate.

Atlas

Suez Canal
1. Egypt
2. Mediterranean and Red Seas
3. Africa

Panama Canal
1. Panama
2. Atlantic and Pacific Oceans
3. South America

Search Engine/Encyclopedia:
1. Elizabeth Jane Cochrane
2. 1869
3. 1914

Fact Find #17: Octopus in the Post Office

Thesaurus:
1. Possible answers include *clever*, *original*, and *inventive*.
2. Answers will vary.

Images:
The post office is very small. There would not be enough room.

Metric Converter:
1. 164
2. 9.8

Atlas:
1. Yes
2. Yes

Search Engine/Encyclopedia:
1. Yes

Fact Find #18: Organs You Can't Play

Thesaurus:
1. Possible answers include *essential*, *necessary*, *key*, *required*, and *needed*.
2. Answers will most likely include a ball, a glove, and a bat.

Calculator:
1. 103,680 beats per day
2. 37,843,200 beats per year
3. His numbers were too low.

Search Engine/Encyclopedia:
1. False, ~~heart~~, skin.
2. True
3. False, ~~two~~, one

Images: the heart

Fact Find #19: The Greatest Inventor

Dictionary:
1. exclusive or sole right granted by a government to an inventor to manufacture, use, or sell an invention for a certain number of years
2. Yes

Search Engine/Encyclopedia:
1. False. Morgan was born in Paris, Kentucky.
2. False. Edison was born in Milan, Ohio.
3. False. The largest is Lake Superior.

Calculator:
1. 86 years
2. 84 years
3. Morgan lived longer.

Fact Find #20: Where Are the Strawberries?

Dictionary:
1. easy to get or use
2. C

Atlas:
1. south
2. about 88

Temperature Converter:
1. 60.8°–73.4°F
2. 39.2°–53.6°F
3. Fahrenheit
4. Celsius, because those temperatures describe warm sunny days and cool nights.

Images:
1. No
2. No

Search Engine/Encyclopedia:
1. fruit
2. vegetable
3. vegetable
4. vegetable

Fact Find #21: Eggs, Tears, and the Nile

Dictionary:
1. Possible answers include *strong*, *difficult*, or *requiring or using great exertion*.

Temperature Converter:
1. 89°F
2. 94.1°F

Atlas: No, Sudan and South Sudan are in between.

Search Engine/Encyclopedia:
1. False, ~~mammals~~, reptiles.
2. False. The Mediterranean is where it empties out.
3. True

Fact Find #22: Enough Rice?

Thesaurus:

1. Possible answers include *huge*, *large*, *tremendous*, and *gigantic*.

2. D

Images: Yes

Calculator:

(Answers are written in this format: "square number : grains of rice." For example, "3 : 4" means that there were 4 grains of rice on Square #3.)

1. 4 : 8; 5 : 16; 6 : 32; 7 : 64; 8 : 128; 9 : 256; 10 : 512; 11 : 1,024; 12 : 2,048; 13 : 4,096; 14 : 8,192; 15 : 16,384; 16 : 32,768; 17 : 65,536; 18 : 131,072; 19 : 262,144; 20 : 524,288

Sum of all squares = 18,446,744,073,709,551,615

Fact Find #23: Scared Stiff

Dictionary:

1. You become so frightened that you are unable to move or think.

2. B

Images:

1. The drawing should show a creature with 2 body parts and 8 legs.

2. large abdomen

Calculator:

1. Answers will vary.

2. Yes

3. No

4. Yes

5. Yes

Translator:

1. queen

2. D

Fact Find #24: A Day Longer than a Year

Thesaurus:

1. D

Images:

1. Yes

2. 3rd: Earth, 4th: Mars

Calculator: Answers will vary.

Fact Find #25: Seaworthy Sale?

Thesaurus:

1. ship, boat, tanker

2. cup, bowl, mug

Atlas:

1. True

2. True

Currency Converter: Answers depend on the current exchange rate.

Search Engine/Encyclopedia:

1. 4th

2. Indian

3. bow — front

   stern — back

   port — left

   starboard — right